LONG DISTANCE WALKS IN
NORTH AFRICA

MATT DICKINSON

SERIES EDITOR JOHN CLEARE

The Crowood Press

First published in 1991 by
The Crowood Press Ltd
Ramsbury, Marlborough
Wiltshire SN8 2HR

British Library Cataloguing in Publication Data

Dickinson, Matt
  Long distance walks in North Africa.
  1. Walking recreations
  I. Title
  796.510961

ISBN 1 85223 523 3

Picture Credits
All photographs are by the author unless otherwise credited;
all maps by Don Sargeant; all line illustrations by Julia Harman.

Typeset by Avonset, Midsomer Norton, Bath
Printed and bound in Great Britain by BPCC Hazell Books, Aylesbury

Contents

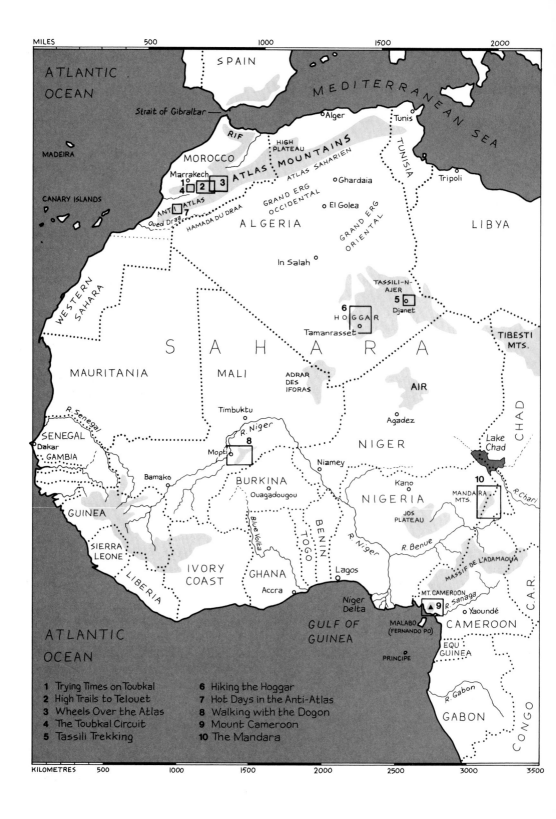

MILES · 500 · 1000 · 1500 · 2000

ATLANTIC OCEAN

SPAIN

MEDITERRANEAN SEA

Strait of Gibraltar

Alger
Tunis

MADEIRA

RIF
MOROCCO

HIGH PLATEAU
ATLAS MOUNTAINS
ATLAS SAHARIEN

Tripoli

CANARY ISLANDS

Marrakech
1 □ 2 □ 3 □
4 □
ANTI-ATLAS
7 □
Oued Draa
HAMADA DU DRAA

Ghardaia

GRAND ERG OCCIDENTAL

El Golea

LIBYA

ALGERIA

GRAND ERG ORIENTAL

In Salah

WESTERN SAHARA

TASSILI-N-AJER
5 □
Djanet

TIBESTI MTS.

MAURITANIA

MALI

6 □
HOGGAR
Tamanrasset

ADRAR DES IFORAS

AIR

S A H A R A

Timbuktu
R. Niger
8 □
Mopti

Agadez

NIGER

Lake Chad

CHAD

R. Senegal

SENEGAL
Dakar
GAMBIA

Bamako

BURKINA
Ouagadougou

Niamey

Kano

NIGERIA
JOS PLATEAU

MANDARA MTS.
10 □

R. Chari

GUINEA

SIERRA LEONE

Blue Volta

BENIN
TOGO

R. Niger

R. Benue

MASSIF DE L'ADAMAOUA

C.A.R.

LIBERIA

IVORY COAST

GHANA
Accra

Lagos

Niger Delta

MT. CAMEROON
▲ 9 □
R. Sanaga
Yaoundé

CAMEROON

ATLANTIC OCEAN

GULF OF GUINEA

MALABO (FERNANDO PO)

PRINCIPE

EQU. GUINEA

R. Gabon

CONGO

GABON

1 Trying Times on Toubkal
2 High Trails to Telouet
3 Wheels Over the Atlas
4 The Toubkal Circuit
5 Tassili Trekking
6 Hiking the Hoggar
7 Hot Days in the Anti-Atlas
8 Walking with the Dogon
9 Mount Cameroon
10 The Mandara

KILOMETRES · 500 · 1000 · 1500 · 2000 · 2500 · 3000 · 3500

Preface

'Travel' wrote Francis Bacon nearly four hundred years ago, 'is a part of education.' It is indeed, but it is also far more than that. Many see the burgeoning travels of today's common man as an important key to international understanding and future world harmony. Others — more pessimistic, yet perhaps more perceptive — see the profligate scatter of the tourist dollar as enriching local economies while despoiling subtle cultures and eroding fragile environments. There is much truth in both views. Travel is surely a two-edged sword.

Thus we who travel and enjoy the wild places — at risk by their very definition — bear a heavy responsibility. It is up to us to do the right thing, to set the right example, and back at home thoughtfully to champion the cause of the wilderness. It is all too easy to kill the goose that lays the golden eggs.

Leave nothing but footprints, take nothing but photographs must be our guiding principle. The conservation ethos may seem out of place in impoverished regions whose inhabitants are struggling even to subsist, but in these very regions where cause and effect form a vicious and ever-tightening circle, the environment is often at greatest risk. It is sobering to realize that the Sahara was once well-watered savannah and that North Africa was the granary of the Roman Empire. Ecological historians claim the goat as a crucial cause of the still encroaching sands: for what will they blame the wilderness traveller in centuries to come?

This book is another in our on-going series covering LONG DISTANCE WALKS and ADVENTURE TREKS. We hope to encourage the discerning traveller to undertake and enjoy adventurous journeys eschewing mechanical transport — treks, hikes, walks, call them what you will — through many of the best locations for such activities among the world's wild places. Typically the routes traverse mountain or upland country for obvious reasons, and with difficulties and commitments to suit most tastes.

Most travel books fall into one of two categories. Some are guidebooks pure and simple, usually useful and at best even interesting if hardly a 'good read'. Others are narrative accounts, readable, fascinating, often extremely entertaining, but typically disdainfully ignoring any desire of readers to repeat the journey themselves. Hopefully this series embraces something of both, entertaining and enthusing — albeit itchy-footedly — while pointing the traveller on his or her way with first-hand practical advice and crucial information.

Africa has always fascinated our author, Matt Dickinson. He lived in Nigeria as a child and after reading archaeology and anthropology at university, has travelled widely throughout the 'Dark Continent', particularly in off-the-tourist-track areas, and has guided professionally in the High Atlas. Although his work today as a film-maker and producer often takes him to remote areas of the world, north-western Africa and its arid mountains are still his favourite stamping ground. Indeed, he counts the Touareg nomads — the subject of his university dissertation — among his special friends.

For this book he has selected ten exciting itineraries in this vast, empty, exciting yet little-travelled corner of Africa, much of it suprisingly accessible from Europe or North America. Travel with him, share his adventures and maybe one day make a journey there yourself.

John Cleare

5

Introduction

The *Michelin Map No. 153, Africa (North and West)* — reissued as *Michelin 953* — is the most romantic map in the world. It captivated my imagination from the first moment I saw it, at the age of 12, in a library. It covers the entire Sahara desert in loving detail. Where there is an oasis, the *153* shows elegantly drawn palm trees. Where there are sand dunes, the *153* becomes a wonderful bright yellow. Close inspection even reveals textured artwork indicating in which direction a range of dunes is moving.

The map shows tracks that have never known any imprint other than a camel's hoof. It shows where ancient rock engravings can be found. It marks French Foreign Legion forts and takes the trouble to give the location of the loneliest tree in the world, the 'Arbre du Ténéré', in central Niger. How extraordinary that a map which covers 26 African countries sees fit to mark the position of a single tree. Other idiosyncratic oddities of the map are tracks which finish in a dead end at a random point. So who travels them? And why do they stop in the middle of nowhere?

Should you happen to arrive at Wau en Namus, an isolated well in southern Libya, the *153* will again be invaluable. Not only will it tell you that the well is hard to find, but it informs the thirsty desert traveller that the water is brackish. At the well of Termit Sud in Niger the water is good but you will need a rope 80ft (24m) long to gain access to it. On occasions I have arrived at a well and put the map to the test. It rarely fails. In one instance the water was marked 'eau leger. salée à 3m'. I pulled up a bucket of water and measured the length of rope required to reach the water. It was 10ft 6in (3m 28cm). And then I tasted the water. Sure enough, there was the clearly detectable tang of salt. Now that's what I call a map!

My interest in the Sahara increased when I read classic tales of journeys across the region. They included historical works such as Mungo Park's *Travels into the interior of Africa*, and contemporary books like Richard Tench's *Forbidden Sands*. It only made my infatuation worse. I set out to explore the lines on this mystical map for myself and in the subsequent 14 years of travelling there has scarcely been one year in which I have not set foot in some forgotten corner of the *Michelin 153*. Algeria and Mali came first, and later I researched my anthropology dissertation at a nomadic village in Niger. More recently, I have had the good fortune to travel some of the lesser known tracks of Libya and Chad. Increasingly, though, I found myself drawn to the mountains of this part of Africa. The experience of walking through remote areas is doubly interesting in a region where so few people see anything other than the view through the windscreen of a landrover. Some of the regions are well known, like the High Atlas and the Hoggar. Others, such as the Bandiagara, Tassili and Mandara will be new names to many who read this book. All of the mountains described can be found on the *Michelin 153*.

Five sections in this book are devoted to trekking in the High Atlas and Anti Atlas Mountains of Morocco, for it is here that the giants of north-west Africa are to be found. Recent years have seen a massive surge of interest in this area, no doubt because amongst the arid peaks of the Atlas are some of the finest treks in the African continent. Also, the region is easily and cheaply reached from Europe. The other five hikes belong less to the mainstream of recognized African mountain walks, but describe areas which are fascinating to explore on foot. Overland travellers and backpackers so often rush through these regions of Africa, when a few

Typical footpath through the Mandara. Trails like this link all the villages and go on for miles.

days' walking would prove a highlight of the trip. Some of the walks may seem like random journeys through unmapped areas, but I make no excuses for that. I believe this is the essence of trekking — to set off with a backpack and not know where you will spend the night gives a walk a tang of excitement which is hard to recreate on an organized tour.

Most importantly, all of these walks will bring you into contact with the people who live their day-to-day lives amongst the mountains of Africa. The Touareg, the Dogon and the Berbers are fascinating tribes with whom it is worth spending some time. Their lives are often dictated by the precarious balance of nature in marginal lands, and being sensitive to this will enhance not only your experience of them, but their impression of you. It is an important point that neatly ties in with something a French traveller once told me: 'Africa is not a place to go if you just want to walk . . . it is a place to get to know Africans!'

Trying Times on Toubkal

If it is possible to have an accidental attraction to a mountain then mine is to North Africa's highest, Toubkal. Over 12 years of a classic love-hate relationship I have yomped, trekked, scrambled, climbed, and snowholed on it, and cursed my way up its unending screes so many times that I have genuinely lost count. I have also been ill on it, got drunk on it, been frozen on it, given an 85-year-old woman a piggy back up it, and swear blind each time that I will never set foot on its rubble-strewn slopes again. Like an embarrassing friend one keeps meeting in the street, Toubkal is unavoidable. Somehow it always lures me back. Strangely, I never plan to return but find myself drawn as if by a magnetic force. Stranger still is that despite the experiences I have described, Toubkal is without doubt my favourite mountain.

The first time I saw Toubkal is a moment I will never forget. Packed into an ancient minibus I was one of 12 members of a school climbing expedition to the High Atlas. It was 1978 and I was 17 years old. The excitement that had been building up amongst the group as we trundled slowly down through France and Spain was at fever pitch as we pulled out of Marrakesh and headed due south. It was a perfect spring day. On either side of the road the olive groves and orange tree orchards were coming to life. Hooded figures wrapped against the cold were riding to work on donkeys and mules to tend the trees and clear the precious irrigation channels that run amongst them. Here and there small groups of men were huddled over fires for warmth.

Suddenly a shout went up from the front of the minibus. We craned forward and then there they were, suspended above the delicate layer of pink dust which so often shrouds the plain of Marrakesh – Toubkal and the highest peaks of the Atlas stood huddled in conference, perfectly white with late season snow. It was more like a vision than a view. Although we had already crossed the Pyrenees and the Sierra Nevada on our journey to Morocco, they paled by comparison with what we saw before us. I thought then, and still do, that the sight of the High Atlas across the Marrakesh plains is one of the world's classic mountain views. They seemed impossibly high. The thought that we should soon be attempting the highest peak amongst them was terrifying. Foreshortened by distance, every face and gully, every crack and summit seemed sheer. In fact the whole range looked as if it rose from the dead flat desert plain like a solid single wall of vertical rock over 13,123ft (4,000m) high. Since none of us had any climbing experience outside Britain, this prompted understandably nervous reactions and not a few sleepless nights. Would we, 10 inexperienced schoolboys, and two semi-experienced teachers, be up to it? We stopped the vehicle and got out to take photographs. I still remember the tight knot of excitement and fear as, consulting a map, we identified Toubkal. It was no longer a name to be pored over in the cosy safety of a

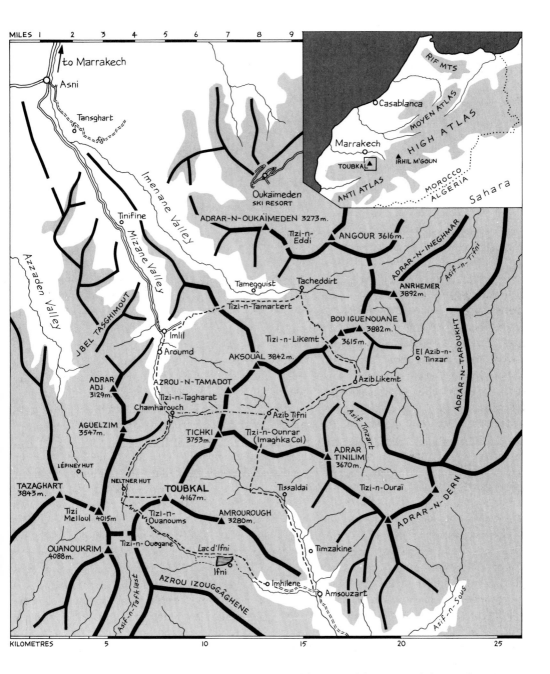

to Marrakech
Asni
Tansghart

RIF MTS
Casablanca
MOYEN ATLAS
Marrakech
HIGH ATLAS
TOUBKAL ▲ IRHIL M'GOUN ▲
ANTI ATLAS
MOROCCO
ALGERIA
Sahara

Imenane Valley
Tinifine
Oukaïmeden
SKI RESORT
ADRAR-N-OUKAÏMEDEN 3273m.
Tizi-n-Eddi
ANGOUR 3616m.
ADRAR-N-INEGHMAR
Azif-n-Tifni

Azzaden Valley
Mizane Valley
Tamegguist
Tacheddirt
ANRHEMER 3892m.

JBEL TASGHIMOUT
Imlil
Aroumd
Tizi-n-Tamartert
BOU IGUENOUANE 3882m.
Tizi-n-Likemt
3615m.
El Azib-n-Tinzar

ADRAR ADJ 3129m.
AZROU-N-TAMADOT
AKSOUAL 3842m.
Azib Likemt
ADRAR-N-TAROUKHT

Tizi-n-Tagharat
Chamharouch
Azib Tifni
Asif Tinzart

AGUELZIM 3547m.
TICHKI 3753m.
Tizi-n-Ounrar (Imaghka Col)
ADRAR TINILIM 3670m.

LÉPINEY HUT
NELTNER HUT
Tissaldai
Tizi-n-Ouraï
ADRAR-N-DERN

TAZAGHART 3843m.
TOUBKAL 4167m.

Tizi Melloul 4015m.
Tizi-n-Ouanoums
AMROUROUGH 3280m.

OUANOUKRIM 4088m.
Tizi-n-Ouagane
Lac d'Ifni
Timzakine

Asif-n-Tafk last
Ifni
AZROU IZOUGGAGHENE
Imhilene
Amsouzart
Asif-n-Sous

geography classroom. It was up there waiting for us, coated in snow and ice. After 10 days of lesser walks and climbs, a few of us would be chosen to climb it. I wanted more than anything to be one of that team.

First we had to survive the cliff-hanging switchbacks and hairpins of the road to Asni. What is it about Moroccan truck drivers that gives them a divine conviction that nothing can ever be coming the other way? Several times we were pushed to the edge of the road with a hair-raising 1,000ft (300m) drop on one side and the

9

manic smile of a death-wish truck driver on the other. Below us the Assif-n-Ighighagene played host to the burnt-out skeletons of those cars and trucks which had not been so lucky. Leaving the plains far behind, the road climbed rapidly, gaining nearly 1,600ft (500m) in height after the village of Taddert before levelling off again on the small flat plateau where Asni is located.

Asni is an inevitable stopping-off point for those heading for Toubkal and opinions on it vary. We arrived that first time on a market day when the place was alive. Hundreds of traders and hopeful buyers from the surrounding villages were busy bargaining for fresh meat and livestock, whilst brightly clad women sat patiently by their wares — a few walnuts, fresh mint, or a mound of potatoes. We saw the good side of Asni. On days when there is no market it changes its character completely and becomes a dusty, scrappy roadside stop for truck drivers on their way to the Tizi'n Test pass. Hustlers and 'salesmen' make life a misery with their relentless attempts to sell fossils and hashish to gullible travellers.

Just past Asni a tatty sign points travellers towards Imlil. This is the beginning of the jeep track to the Toubkal trekking area. It is a track that penetrates right into the heart of the High Atlas range and is probably the most popular route amongst newcomers and experienced alike. Although flash floods often wreak havoc on the track it is normally quickly repaired by working gangs from the villages, and it is not usually necessary to have a four-wheel drive vehicle unless there is deep snow. Then comes the first chance to see at close hand the real secret which enables the Berbers to scrape a living from these barren and arid hills — the terraces. No one knows how old they are but they are the only means of cultivation on the steep slopes of the High Atlas. Each one may be planted with a different crop and owned by a different family, but out of the confusion a village

can feed itself in all but the hardest of years. Roving herds of goats and sheep are sent far out into the mountains in search of fodder, and in this way the Berber diet is supplemented with a little meat.

By the time our old minibus had coughed and spluttered its way into the stone-walled square at Imlil we had gained a further 1,550ft (485m) in height since Asni and now stood at 5,413ft (1,650m) above sea level. We unloaded our mound of equipment into the French Alpine Club refuge and set about organizing ourselves for the walking and climbing to come. The next day we set off at dawn, 10 excited schoolboys, two teachers trying hard not to look nervous, and a couple of mules who had seen it all a hundred times before. The great expedition had begun!

The 10 days that followed were a perfect introduction to the joys, and occasional miseries, of walking. Within a couple of days we were blistered and footsore, and many of the group fell sick with stomach upsets, having unwisely sampled the less hygienic wares on offer from the stalls of Marrakesh. But we kept to our plans regardless of who was ill. 'Casualties' were left behind in villages to recover, being picked up at a later stage. In this way we made good time and were able to make an ascent of Angour at 11,863ft (3,600m), based out of the French Alpine Club refuge at Tacheddirt. A few days later we crossed the Tizi'n Mzik at 8,740ft (2,600m) and had some excellent ice gully climbing in the high valley above the Lepiney hut. We had deliberately chosen the spring season for the high level snow and we were not disappointed . . . the conditions were ideal, so far.

By a process of natural selection the expedition divided into three groups: those who were not fit enough to try Toubkal; those who were fit enough but did not particularly want to try; and four of us who were going to try it whatever state we were in. The rest of the expedition was packed off in the minibus for a tour of the

From there the trail levelled off as it divided into various routes, none markedly better than the rest, to cross the gravel and boulder-strewn flood plain of the valley bottom. Eventually, after about ½ mile (1km), it climbed rapidly up towards Sidi Charamouch. On the right-hand side the slopes of Adrar Adj begin their journey up to the summit at 10,265ft (3,200m). On the left are the flanks of Akoual and Azrou-n-Tamadot at 12,020ft (3,600m). Low-lying scrubby trees and bushes dot the valleysides, showing much evidence of heavy grazing by goats. We stopped for chocolate rations and put on snow gaiters for the first time during our time in the High Atlas. Out of the gloom, a couple of muleteers emerged carrying pilgrims down from the pilgrim shrine at Sidi Charamouch. During holy festivals there are many hundreds, perhaps even thousands, of pilgrims who make this journey, travelling from as far away as Casablanca or Fez. City dwellers for the most part, they tend to find the trek hard going and the muleteers at Imlil do a brisk trade in hauling them up to the shrine. On the ascent the pilgrims place stones on top of the larger boulders, creating small cairns that can consist of many hundreds of stones. The track climbed steadily, often zigzagging back on itself but always keeping to the left or east bank of the river. When the clouds parted and visibility improved the river was revealed below, plunging into a series of deep pools which we had been told were excellent for swimming, although the prospect of a swim in those conditions was not one we relished.

Toubkal ascent in winter.

prettier southern oasis towns whilst our small team stayed in Imlil to prepare the ropes and equipment for the next day's departure to the Neltner hut at 10,521ft (3,200m). We found a thick layer of snow had fallen overnight when we abandoned the relative warmth of the Imlil refuge at 6.30 a.m. A metallic white light indicated the direction in which the sun was vainly trying to rise, but the Mizane valley was plunged into a gloomy, cloud-laden mood. Fresh snow fell in the gusts of wind. The weather had been getting increasingly cold over the previous days but this was a definite change for the worse. Although the visibility began to fall we had no trouble in following the track as it snaked up through frozen terraces and walnut groves towards the village of Aroumd.

Battle-hardened by the training period that had gone before, we had become used to carrying heavy canvas backpacks. Inside each one was a sleeping bag, 'bivvy' bag, change of clothing, half a 'Vango' Force Ten tent, five days of 'compo' army rations (mostly in tins), camping gas cylinders and mess tins for cooking, plastic mug, Swiss army knife, map, compass, whistle, and a few personal extras such as Kendal mint cake and a book. Strapped to the

The Berbers are the guardians of the High Atlas, and the best mountain guides in Africa.

exterior were crampons, karrimat, and ice axe. Distributed between us were the ropes and climbing hardware. We thought we were pretty macho but learned the truth a short distance from the shrine when four Frenchwomen rushed past us carrying packs which looked twice the size and weight of ours. And they were carrying skis too!

A few hours after leaving Imlil we were at Sidi Charamouch. Unless you are a pilgrim, there is little about the place that could be called attractive. It lies at the confluence of two valleys, the one to the right climbs up towards the Neltner hut while the left branch is a very steep climb up to the Tizi-n-Tagharat from where access can be gained to the eastern approaches to Toubkal. A few modest 'shops' lurk in Charamouch for the unwary hiker who has not learned quite how bad stale Moroccan chocolate biscuits taste. When we asked, very politely, if we could see inside the shrine, we were told, equally politely, that we could not. 'There are sick people inside' said the guardian, 'we must respect the sick.'

However, we paused just long enough for an orange drink and to chat with members of a Scottish climbing expedition who were on their way down. They were in a fine mood. 'How was Toubkal?' we asked. 'A piece of cake!'

Leaving the shrine, the track rapidly gains height and then continues up the valley towards the Neltner hut. A thin line of footprints from those who had already passed that day acted as a guide. The snow was deep now, and drifting heavily in some places. Once or twice one of our party would unwittingly step on the solid ice of a frozen spring below and slide down the slope before arresting his fall with an ice axe. Our days practising on ice in Scotland were proving well spent. Although we could hear the muffled roar of the river coursing below us, we could not see it. A bridge of snow and ice obscured it completely from view. The weather now seemed to be deteriorating as we climbed. The snow fell thickly around us, settling on our woolly hats and giving the walk an added element of excitement. We knew that Toubkal would be challenging enough for us without bad conditions to contend with. If the wind increased we would be in for some interesting climbing. Privately, we all wanted drama!

The Neltner hut finally came into view after a moderately hard three-hour slog from Sidi Charamouch. We collapsed into the warm interior. The scene inside was one that climbers and trekkers know well; a room packed with bodies, gear and maps, alive with conversation and the sound of cooking. A stack of skis was propped against the hut wall, while piles of climbing rope and other hardware were hanging from every peg. A warm fug of cigarette smoke and steam filled the room. The smell of boots, sweat and coffee permeated the atmosphere. French, German and Italian merged into an incomprehensible muddle of sound. It was a cosy scene.

The guardian and a couple of Berber helpers from Aroumd were busy boiling water and trying to keep the place clean. A French climber advised us not to drink the water in the refuge as it was polluted. Many of the occupants who had been in the hut for a couple of days had become sick. I wondered why this was but realized later that the water supply came from roughly the same area that the hut's occupants used as an open-air latrine. The talk was of the weather, with everyone having their own theory as to how it would develop. Looking out of the window at the steady fall of snow, most agreed it was not likely to get any better in the short term. Meanwhile we cooked a stodgy meal and washed it down with plenty of tea before packing up and preparing to leave the refuge. Our plan had always been to camp out wherever we could and the Neltner hut was in any case far too overcrowded.

Every single mattress in the upstairs dormitory was occupied by two people. They were packed in like sardines. Nevertheless, it was not easy to abandon all that warmth and security and step out into the freezing late afternoon. The guardian warned us that a blizzard might blow up during the night but our group agreed to continue. As we left, we ran into a Canadian being sick outside the refuge. He looked really ill. I asked him why he did not return to Imlil and he replied that he was too weak to walk. He kicked the wall of the refuge, 'Bloody place!' he muttered, 'I'm the prisoner of Neltner!' We gave him some drugs from our medical kit in the hope of relieving his illness. The last sight of him as we walked out into the snow was of a bent figure retching on an empty stomach, cursing the world.

There were still three hours of daylight left but we soon found we were very tired from the day's trek. Finding a small patch of level ground, we pitched camp for the night. At dawn the next day we packed the gear and started up the steep face that rises to the east of the Neltner. Apart from the wind, which was blowing even stronger than before, the only sound was of the muffled plod of cramponed boots into the snow and the rhythmical crunch as the ice axe tips went in.

From below, this face had looked like a quick ascent but, with the lead climber cutting steps all the way, it was slow work. Even with down-filled gloves my hands were numb with the cold. The Neltner hut was invisible, since clouds were now accompanying the snow. Looking ahead, it seemed we were about to straddle a col but a glance at the map showed this to be a false impression. It was in fact the lip of the entrance to the great western couloir of Toubkal. Entering this natural amphitheatre we paused to take in the conditions. The Mizane valley was no longer visible and with every minute that passed the weather worsened. We ate chocolate and mint cake and discussed our plans. Normally, we would have continued up into the couloir and made for the summit, but the visibility was now so bad that we could not even see the walls of the gorge. The threatening wind finally made up its mind to go full throttle and became a

View from the summit of Toubkal.

blizzard. Even with a compass it would be folly to go higher.

The decision was made. We would have to find somewhere to pitch the tents and sit out the storm. There was no question of going back to the Neltner hut because our tracks would have been obliterated by the snow. No really flat ground was to be found but we excavated a rough platform from the snow which would have to suffice. Erecting the tents was the next problem. The fly sheets flew like sails as soon as they were unpacked. We wrestled them into position and pushed the pegs deep into the snow to give the tents the best chance of staying up. The rucksacks were pushed inside (along with plenty of snow) and we followed, grateful for the protection and warmth. We had never experienced a storm like this. All our previous storm encounters had been in the highlands of Scotland but this was altogether more impressive. The guy ropes thrummed and sang as

the wind tried every trick to bring down the tents. At times, the front would sag and bend alarmingly, only to spring resolutely back into shape before the next assault. The howling increased dramatically as the day wore on into the afternoon.

The couloir acted as a natural wind funnel, shaping and moulding its forces into a concentrated wall of fury. Our respect for the resilience of the canvas tents was growing. They are heavy and bulky but they really can take punishment when asked. If they could survive this battering, they could survive anything. We lapsed into an uneasy wait, taking snatched opportunities for sleep and reading such literary gems as *The Guns of Navarone* and *Zen and the Art of Motorcycle Maintenance*. There was little conversation save the odd shouted exchange between tents:

'You alright over there?'

'No. We're dead. You alright over there?'

'No. We're dead too. What's it like over there?'

'Windy. What's it like over there?'

'Windy.'

Wit was not a strong point of our little expedition!

The night seemed interminably long and the severity of the storm never eased. Every two hours one of us would perform the unattractive task of going out into the cold and attempting to clear the drifted snow from the tents. Whenever it was my turn I looked around for some of the surrounding slopes, but it was a continuous 'whiteout', with nothing but blank walls of falling snow and low cloud in sight. We decided to squeeze into one tent for a 'powwow'. There was no sign of a break in the storm, and a couple of our team were feeling ill. It is often during enforced waits, when the day-to-day action of continous trekking is unavoidably halted, that illness strikes. The decision was to give it one more day in the tents – if it was looking better in the morning we would attempt the summit, if not we would retreat to Imlil. Time was running out.

The day dragged on and sleep was the most attractive prospect. By now the canvas tent walls were soaked through with spindrift, and being pushed up against them our sleeping bags were constantly damp. The night seemed even longer than the one before because we had no torch batteries left to read by. There was nothing to do but listen to the storm whistling around us. At least there was no longer any danger of the tents being blown away because they were now hemmed in under the snow. We gave up going out to dig them free. It was too much effort. By morning a quick glance through the tent flaps

A Berber guide prepares tea.

told us all we needed to know – the conditions were the same. The whiteout blizzard continued. Two hours later we decided to abandon our Toubkal attempt and get off the mountain. It was deeply depressing but we had no choice because our rendezvous with the rest of the expedition was only two days away.

When we started packing up the kit I was shocked by how weak I felt. The altitude of 11,482ft (3,500m) coupled with two days spent immobile in the tents had weakened us all considerably. The awful task of digging out the tents began. Each one was anchored into the ground by frozen snow and rock-hard ice. The pegs were gripped to the extent that only an ice axe could chip them out. Encumbered by the bulky overgloves, and stiff with cold, we fumbled and wrestled with the task. It took over an hour to get the tents released. The canvas was impossible to handle, for it had become rigidly stiff and difficult to fold. One flysheet remained stuck fast in the ice, its guy ropes embedded deep in a drift. As we began to dig it free a particularly ferocious blast of wind whipped it into the air and a jagged rip appeared in the canvas. For another 15 minutes we tried to extricate it from the ice without more damage, but the thing was stuck fast. We made the decision to abandon it on the mountain. We were all exhausted and we could not spare another ounce of energy to dig out a piece of redundant equipment.

The descent began through the white wall of snow. Sometimes a black rock would loom out of the haze, otherwise it was difficult to tell which way was up or down. I fell awkwardly on the ice deceived by the whiteout into seeing a foothold which was further away than it looked. On several occasions we stopped ourselves falling with ice axe arrests. The slope down to the Neltner was treacherous, with frequent ice patches lurking beneath the snow. Two hours later we were at the safety of the Neltner refuge. We thawed out and swapped stories of our experiences with the other trekkers and climbers.

The storm had forced everyone in the area to take cover and, as a result, the refuge was now packed solid with impatient souls waiting for the situation to clear. The conditions inside were rather squalid. We paused just long enough to drink tea and eat dates before shouldering our packs and descending the Mizane valley to Imlil. Whatever disappointment we felt at our failures on Toubkal was tempered by the exhilaration of experiencing the storm. We had definitely made the right decision to abandon a summit attempt and were all a little wiser about the realities of bad weather at high altitude.

The next time I set foot on Toubkal was a couple of years later. It was summer and the mountain presented a very different face from that first abortive attempt. Only a few isolated pockets of dirty snow hid in the shadiest corners. The upper slopes were arid, and baked to oven temperatures by the North African sun. The seasons are hard on the fabric of the High Atlas, and Toubkal has the air of a mountain in the process of crumbling to the ground. Only in the lower valleys that surround the peak is there enough vegetation to attract the goatherds and their animals away from the villages. The older inhabitants remember a time when these valleys were lush with grass and trees. Overgrazing has had a devastating effect on the High Atlas, as elsewhere in North Africa.

Climbing Toubkal presents no problem at all in summer for anyone who is moderately fit. The only tough aspect of the climb is the loose rock and scree which makes the going difficult and tiring. Once the couloir has been gained from the Neltner hut the most common route continues up the right-hand flank on a southeast trajection to the final ridge. This is a fairly exposed area with some alarming drops to the south, but the summit is easily achieved. Once there the walker is rewarded with a superb panoramic vista which takes in almost the entire Toubkal region. When visibility is good, the

Trekking group at dawn on summer ascent of Toubkal.

peaks of the Anti Atlas can be seen far to the south. The only thing which spoils the summit is the ugly triangulation point which attracts some exotic graffiti.

My involvement with Toubkal took a further twist when the adventure tour operators 'Explore Worldwide' posted me there to run a season of treks. It was my job to get people up Toubkal, and the summer seemed to pass in an endless round of permanent scree bashing. Toubkal was mischievous on most of my tours. Twice I had to get group members off the mountain in a hurry when they began to feel the effects of high altitude or were too ill to continue. Once, an ebullient Australian character called Shane drank half a bottle of whisky during an overnight bivouac on the summit, knocked over his water bottle and then moaned all night that he was dehydrated. A burly Norfolk vet threatened to throw him off the mountain and Shane suffered in silence from then on!

Leaving Marrakesh at the end of that long season I was sure I would never set foot on Toubkal again but, sure enough, that mysterious magnetic force worked its spell and in 1989 I was back. This time it was for a mountain bike

journey across the entire High Atlas range. The journey was to be filmed for the Central TV/ National Geographic series *Voyager*. Nick Crane, Chris Bradley and I were the subjects of the film of what turned out to be a spectacular and demanding trip (*see* Wheels over the Atlas, page 29). The climax came when we shouldered the bikes on a freezing cold January morning at the Neltner hut ready to climb to the summit. Since there was deep snow on Toubkal, climbing it with mountain bikes was not entirely sensible. In fact, looking back, it was a thoroughly lunatic thing to do, but at the time it seemed quite natural, and by that stage of the trip we were getting used to the weight of the mountain bike on our backs.

As I panted my way to the summit I thought of all the other trying times I had experienced on Toubkal and realized this was the ultimate — carrying a bicycle 13,670ft (4,100m) in winter! It was a scene which 6.04 million people later witnessed from the comfort of their living rooms. I wondered if this was the last laugh Toubkal would have on me. Surely, I thought (as I crawled to the summit) I would never again return. Would I?

High Trails to Telouet

The central section of the High Atlas range is well worth exploring. Being slightly further from the main cities of the south and more difficult to reach, it attracts fewer walkers and climbers than the Toubkal region, and is consequently more enticing. The villages are less influenced by the outside world, while the trails are lonely and sometimes difficult to find. Even

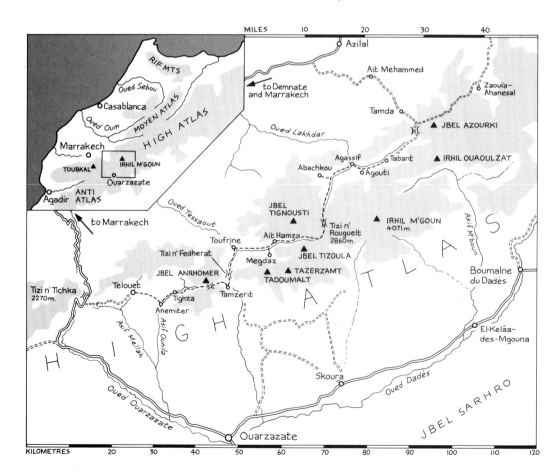

the official maps of the area seem to have been compiled by someone who never managed to get there. The mountains themselves, whilst not matching the cluster of big peaks in the Toubkal region, are nonetheless challenging and wild.

The traditional starting point for one- to two-week hikes in the central High Atlas is the Ait Bou Guemez valley. This is normally reached from Marrakesh by taking the P24 road towards El-Kelaa-des-Srarhna, and branching off east at Tamelet-el-kdima on the S508 route. This is followed to Azilal, where a road heads south to Ait Mohammed, where the climb begins up a dirt track into the Bou Guemez. For those without transport the journey to Bou Guemez can be managed by local buses and shared taxis. The last section is only served by very slow, and packed, market trucks. In fact I used the latter method to trundle into Bou Guemez after two days of uncomfortable travel from Marrakesh. On the way I met an Italian called Remo who was intending to go walking in the area and we agreed to travel together, sharing the cost of food and mules.

The truck from Ait Mohammed had two means of transportation. They involved hanging on to the side, or getting into the back. The younger men chose clinging, whilst cowards like Remo and I took the easy option. The side-clingers had a favourite and rather frustrating habit which only served to remind us how slowly the truck was inching up the switchback mountain. At particular bends in the track they would nonchalantly leap to the ground and walk directly to the next bend. The truck would wheeze and splutter its way about the hillside, taking 5–10 minutes to catch up with them. Walking on they would jeer and clap, before climbing back on to the sides. Thus the journey continued.

Our fellow passengers in the back were heading for the market at Tabant, and many had goods for sale. Fruit, and livestock abounded, while others had truck tyres and boxes of foodstuffs from Azilal. I perched nervously on an oil drum which contained diesel as Remo puffed away on a black tobacco cigarette, one of the many Italian luxuries he had brought with him, as I was to discover over the next days. I struck up a conversation with a youth who knew some English. He nodded approvingly when he heard of our plans: 'Oh yes, you have come to the most beautiful part of Morocco. This is, how do you say, the garden of Eden!' And as we crested the Jbel Azourki flank at the Tizi-n-Tirghist — 8,625ft (2,600m) — it was hard to disagree with him. The Bou Guemez really is one of the most appealing valleys in the whole of the High Atlas.

To the south, the valley is completely protected by the Ighil Mgoun massif, over which no road has ever dared to attempt a crossing. The high point is Ighil-n-Oumsoud at 13,341ft (4,000m), a height which makes it an automatic target by those seeking 4km climbs in the Atlas. The route out of the Bou Guemez to Mgoun takes the Tizi-n-Ait Imi at 9,530ft (2,900m) but by far the majority of those heading for Mgoun do so from the south where access is far easier. Ahead, the market at Tabant was in full swing when we arrived. Donkey convoys were streaming in from every direction as the buyers and sellers got down to the real business of the day. Some offered intricate rugs, woven from camel hair and coloured with natural dyes. Others sat with a heap of dried tomatoes, dates or figs. In small tents men with turbans and beards gossiped, hearing the news from villages in far away valleys. In one particular corner a blacksmith squatted by a charcoal fire with leather bellows at his feet. Young children walked amongst the stalls, gazing wide-eyed at the goods on offer. Plastic wellingtons were much in demand, those in bright yellow being the most popular.

Remo ordered food — a couple of 'tagine' bowls — and we sat at a low bench mopping up the stew with fresh bread. There were generous lumps of meat to chew on, always the sign of a

The Glaoui Kasbah at Telouet.

prosperous region. Hopeful vendors came up with leather trinkets and lumps of 'precious' stone which looked to us like common or garden quartz. A woman stumbled past carrying a hay-stack on her back, and a group of children gathered round to watch the free show we were providing. Remo amused them with sleight of hand tricks with his cigarette lighter, making it appear from their ears and then vanish into thin air. Within minutes, adults also gathered to watch. I was beginning to wonder if travelling with Remo was such a good idea. I pulled him away from his audience and we went to find an 'auberge'. Eventually we found someone who knew where it was and half an hour later we were ushered into what must be the best-kept inn of the High Atlas. The rooms were clean and well kept, the atmosphere somehow stran-gely European for such a remote spot.

After a welcoming glass of hot mint tea we spread out our maps on the terrace to discuss possible trekking routes for the coming days. The possibilities were endless but wherever we ended up had to be at a road head so we could get transport to Marrakesh. I mentioned to Remo a previous route I had trekked when I had set out from the ancient Kasbah of Telouet. Since he had read much about the former stronghold of the Glaoui family, he was as in-terested to get there as I was keen to explore more of the villages in the Oued Tessaout. We settled on a journey west. Our first disagreement blew up over the question of mules. Remo did not think hiring them fitted his image. Italian walkers, he told me, carry their gear on their backs! Besides, it was cruel to animals. I pointed out that the mules were only kept alive to carry loads and that if they did not they would be killed. He replied that he could not care less if the mules were dead or alive, which seemed odd from someone so concerned for their welfare a moment before. I said there was no point in carrying a load when there were beasts of burden to do it for us. He replied that that was a typical English approach.

The next morning we left on our walk westwards. My backpack was in the pannier of a very fit-looking mule which had been hired cheaply at the market. Remo carried his bulging rucksack on his back, trying hard to look as if he was enjoying it. The conditions were perfect, just a fresh spring breeze in the air and a dusting of snow on the higher peaks of the Jbel Tizal away to the north. The streams and irrigation channels were running full with meltwater and the fields looked green and lush with early season shoots of barley and maize. Out of the ornate ironwork windows of the richer dwellings we caught the occasional glimpse of a woman's face. Children stood on the roofs yelling, without any serious hope, for pens and sweets. The morning passed pleasantly as we walked through the settlements that line the broad and fertile valley floor watered by the Assif-n-Ait Bou Goumez. Each village — Ait Ziri, Talsnant, Agouti, and Aguersif — epitomized the rural beauty of the High Atlas.

After a short climb we dropped to a wide track to Aguersif. A jeep track is actually marked on the 1:100,000 'Azilal' map connecting this village to the north, but we never saw any vehicles and the track was in many places washed away. The remains of destroyed bridges at many of the river crossings of the Atlas were a testimony to the ferocious flash floods that occur at certain times of the year. Passing Aguersif we continued up the Oued Lakhdar, crossing the river at points where washouts had destroyed the path on our side. I jumped onto my mule for the river crossings. Remo splashed through in his boots and with each subsequent step squelched as we passed Taghoulit and Ighir-

n-Ighrazene, together making slow progress upwards.

At Abachkou we stopped to look for food. On a previous occasion I had been there on market day when the place was packed with traders from the surrounding areas. But when we arrived the souk was dead. Only the stench of rotting bones and the aggressive attentions of scavenging dogs were there to welcome us. Moroccan markets are bad places to be if it is not market day. We had bread and sardines and sat on the grass of a terrace for a break. It was now that Remo chose to reveal a glimpse of the wonders contained within his enormous rucksack. The man was quite simply a mobile delicatessen. First he produced a lengthy Italian salami, followed by a plastic container with olives, and diced peppers in oil. Our muleteer was suspicious of this exotic fare but Remo kindly shared it with me and we ate well. Perhaps this travelling partnership could work after all, I thought, wondering what other goodies might be hidden away in his backpack.

Lunch was followed by a brief nap and then we followed the southerly branch of the three streams which converge at this junction. This heads up, more steeply now, towards the village of Rhougelt. On the way we passed some spectacular villages, clinging to seemingly impossible slopes. In front was the steep ridge line of the Jbel Tarkeddid. This runs at a fairly level height of 11,482ft (3,500m) and forms the watershed between the Ait Bou Goumez and the Oued Tessaout, one of the most significant water courses in the Atlas. It was almost dark when we arrived at Rhougelt, whereupon our muleteer turned quickly back towards Abachkou where he had a cousin. 'What do we do now?' asked Remo. No one appeared to greet us. I had stayed in this village before, but that was years ago, and I could not remember at which house I had stayed. Instead, I just said, 'Don't worry. If we just sit here someone will come and ask us what we're doing and we can ask for somewhere to

Villagers in the Central High Atlas.

stay.' A ragged bunch of dogs sniffed us suspiciously and a couple of children looked on without saying a word. The light was going fast and nobody else seemed to have noticed our arrival. As a so-called expert I was losing credibility by the minute. It got dark. Still no one came. I wandered around the village and called out at a few doors. Some figures could be seen looking out from the courtyard windows but all my signalling was for nothing. Either nobody understood my sign language for 'Can we stay in your cattle shed?', or they just did not like the idea.

Returning to Remo I was forced to admit that we had not found somewhere to stay. He was not best pleased by this news. We decided to go back down to the river where we had seen a mill which looked to have enough space for us to bivouac in that night. Picking our way down by torchlight we met a villager returning from the fields. He was surprised to see us but kindly offered us space in his house overnight. We entered a warm and welcoming room, decorated with the faded photographs of the male members of his family in military uniform. A pair of wooden shutters was open at the end of the room, providing a view across the valley which was illuminated by the silver-green light of an almost full moon. To our delight a 'tagine' arrived and we ate with the hunger that only a full day's walking can create.

At dawn we woke to a selection of 'alarm clocks'. The first was the village cockerel, swiftly followed by the barking of dogs, the baying of mules and, lastly, the beep-beep-beep of Remo's digital wrist-watch. Rice and bread filled our stomachs, and we were on the trail by 9 a.m. It was cold. The valley leading from the village to the Tizi-n-Rhougelt is cut deep into the rock and in the lower stages we found ourselves walking in perpetual shade. In front of us was a 3,280ft (1,000m) climb to the 9,328ft (2,800m) col. Mules can tackle the route but since we had been unable to find one for hire in the village I

was tackling this Italian style, much to Remo's satisfaction.

Every possible inch of ground that could be cultivated was put to use in that narrow defile. Terraces were built on to the steepest slopes, fed by an arterial network of irrigation channels which might have been there for centuries. So marginal is the food-growing potential of these higher villages that some of the 'fields' are smaller than the size of an average bed. The handful of shoots growing in them may represent a week's supply of food or, if that should fail, a week of hunger. We took the utmost care to avoid trampling on a single plant. During the first hour we passed lonely figures toiling on the land. Hooded against the cold by great brown djellabas, they paused to wave before bending again to work. One called us over and told us he had a 'malade'. The problem was a nasty infection on the shin and, it did indeed look extremely painful. Unfortunately these leg infections are very common in the High Atlas and are caused by the hand hoes and mattocks which are used to turn the soil. Manipulated with a scooping motion towards the body, the slightest slip causes a blow to the leg.

The wound was dirty. It is not unknown for the Berbers to daub dung on to such a cut as a cure. Remo produced a medical kit and we cleaned the injury and dressed it with iodine and a bandage. We told the man that if it grew any worse he must get a doctor for antibiotics, but he protested it would take three days to get to the nearest pharmacy and that the drugs would be expensive. Remo gave the man enough dirhams to cover the cost of the drugs and we left him on our journey upwards.

It is encounters like that which provide an altogether different perspective on life in these remote villages — the harder, less attractive reality of struggle against hunger and disease. The vision of rural tranquillity, which is so much a part of the High Atlas, can quickly fade away when you start to scratch beneath the

The Kasbah at Telouet, scene of a disturbing era in Moroccan history.

surface. The climb continued for two and a half hours on easily identifiable tracks. At some points there was a choice between following the stream bed into minor canyons, or skirting around the top on tiny ledges. The first choice was a sure way to get wet feet. The second involved a fruitless climb and the prospect of a fall into the canyon if we lost our balance. Sometimes, clinging onto tufts of vegetation was the only way to make progress without slipping down the slope. How the mules negotiate these obstacles is anyone's guess but they obviously do because frequent piles of dung marked the trail. The track then started to climb in earnest, zigzagging up to the col. We found occasional patches of snow lurking in shady spots, some with rabbit or fox tracks crossing them.

Four hours after leaving the village we crested the Tizi-n-Rhougelt. A large rock was perched at the top and we sat with our backs resting against it looking down the Tessaout valley. There was no sun to illuminate the scene, and it looked altogether more grim than the first glimpse of the Bou Guemez. We were tired from the climb which we had completed with no real rest, but there was no incentive to linger on the col. A wind was beginning to play across the valley from the south, and spindrift came with it. We ate chocolate and nougat from Remo's supply, then started the descent. By late afternoon we had reached Amezri, a major village of the upper Tessaout valley and a crossroads for some of the most important trails across this part of the Atlas. Unlike the experiences of the previous night, our arrival created quite a stir. It was still early in the season, and few trekkers had been seen for months. A young man with a permanent grin and a green track suit asked if we would like to stay for tea.

His father's house was big, possessing a massive walnut wood door decorated with motifs of iron studs. Tea was served from a silver teapot which rested on a three-legged filigree tray from the souk at Marrakesh. Up here we began to get a real sense of the pull of Marrakesh, and of the excitement the name inspires in the remotest forgotten valleys. Our host's uncle was the 'muezzin' who is responsible for summoning people to prayers at the tiny mosque. He allowed us to watch him call from the minaret. The sound echoed around the valley, 'Allah u Akhbar', and worshippers soon began to gather. It was a moving ceremony to witness, and they clearly did not mind that we were there, some of them even giving us chairs and telling us to stay when we showed signs of leaving.

Tired out after the morning climb, it did not take much persuasion to keep us in Amezri for the night. The hospitality was almost embarrassingly lavish. Three separate dishes of couscous, tagine and rice were given us and the 15 villagers who gathered for the evening. Drums were warmed over a fire and the Berbers sang and played far into the night. Long after Remo and I had crawled exhausted into our sleeping bags, the drumming went on, accompanied by laughter and the shrieks of women.

Day three of our walk started with a shower of rain as we left Amezri with about 50 children in tow. They guided us down to the correct path alongside the river which is crossed at strategic points by stepping stones. The day ahead was unusual in that it involved no climb, just a gradual descent alongside the mighty Tessaout. Remo was feeling ill, and was coming down with a stomach problem which subsequently sent him dashing behind rocks and bushes through the day. We took it easy, meandering slowly down the valley and stopping every hour for a 10-minute rest. The river was quite full but not the raging torrent it can become when flash floods or exceptional meltwater levels arrive. I once saw the Tessaout in full flood and witnessed mature trees plucked up by their roots and carried off down the valley like matchsticks. Most of the fields on the valley floor are destroyed on a regular basis and then rebuilt by the patient Berbers.

The Tessaout drops quickly down the nor-thern flanks of the High Atlas and feeds the Lac des Ait Azde before continuing on its journey north to the artificial lake of the Barrage Al Massira, midway between Marrakesh and Casablanca. From there, under a new name (although it must surely be the route of the original Tessaout), the river runs to the sea at Azemmour, making it the longest and biggest of the north-facing rivers draining the High Atlas. By my calculations it is at least 248 miles (400km) in length. I had hoped to make a diversion to Megdaz, one of the most scenic of all the High Atlas villages, but Remo was feeling sick by mid-afternoon so we continued on the main valley route to Toughrene, where the Tessaout is joined by a smaller oued from the south. Toughrene is connected to the outside world by a track and is therefore more sophisticated than many of the villages we had seen over the past days. Since I had a contact there whom I had once hired as a muleteer, we went straight to his house.

Unfortunately he was away in Marrakesh selling tomatoes and potatoes, but his brother recognized me and we stayed for a day while Remo was fed camomile tea to help his recovery. The Berbers have incredible faith in the healing powers of camomile tea (made from flowers picked on the mountains), and I have seen it produce remarkable results in patients. Remo drank gallons of the camomile, and after a slight overnight fever looked much fitter. I spent the time exploring the village and eating couscous with the chief, whose main ambition in life was to visit Paris. On his wall were Air France posters showing the Eiffel Tower and the Champs Elysées. When I asked him if he should first do the Hadj to Mecca he said 'But of course I have done it already! Three times!' As proof he brought out a picture of himself at the holy site.

After his brief illness Remo finally agreed to put his pack on a mule. We left for Tamzrit, the next night stop on the journey, at 10.30 a.m. after a leisurely breakfast of olive oil and hot bread, washed down by the curious sweet coffee

25

Looking south across the Central High Atlas near the village of Megdaz.

of which the Berbers are fond. (I say 'curious' because it invariably has an aftertaste like the aroma of antiseptic liquid – I do not know why, but I can never get used to it.) The route we were now following was the trail up to the low col of the Tizi-n-Fedherat at 7,155ft (2,100m). Attempts have been made to build a jeep track across this pass and until a few years ago it was still possible, if you had a four-wheel drive vehicle and nerves of steel, to cross from Ouarzazate to Toughrene by this route. But successive years of flooding and landslides have made it impassable. I had heard in Toughrene that a French vehicle had made the journey the year before, but looking at the state of the track I doubted it, unless they had virtually built the road as they went along.

We reached the Fedherat pass after a few hours' gentle climbing up the valley. Now we were looking south towards the Sahara desert for the first time, having crossed the final watershed which divides the range. It was fascinating to think the rain that fell on the northern slope behind us would end up flowing into the sea as far away as Casablanca, whereas rain which fell a few yards further south on the other side of the Fedherat would feed down into the Sahara.

Remo opened up his mobile supermarket for lunch and we dined well on salami, tinned pâté and an excellent piece of cheese, while admiring the view to the south where the hazy reds and browns of the Jbel Sahrho were just visible. Also just in sight was a glimpse of reflected sunlight on the Ouarzazate Barrage some 30 miles (48km) away. That night at Tamzrit we slept on a roof beneath the sky. The stars were

Panorama looking north from Lake Tamda.

brilliant, and it was noticeably warmer than the northern reaches of the range. Remo told me his life story in embarrassing detail. The main thrust of it seemed to be the endless conquest of women who then invariably threatened suicide when Remo got bored with them. 'But they never do' he said casually. He worked in a factory that made bath fittings, designing taps.

Witnessing dawn from the comfort of a sleeping bag is one of my favourite moments. Most nights in the High Atlas are actually spent in villages low in the valleys so dawn gets lost behind the peaks. But from Tamzrit it was spectacular to look out across the southern flanks of the range as the sun rose in a burst of scarlet and yellow. Even Remo was impressed. From here we climbed steeply up the westward track which heads to Jbel Tamadla. It was hard going, with

deep scree to contend with on the zigzag bends. Even in these conditions, and carrying a heavy load, the mule could easily outpace us. Trying to go as fast as a mule is a big mistake in the High Atlas. Only the Berbers can do it.

The muleteer turned back at the top of the climb when we were able to look down into the Tamda valley. It was too steep, he said, for the mule to descend. He had a point; it was steep, and quite a bit of snow still lay on the ground. We went down fast, into the dead-end valley which is formed between the Jbel-n-Anghomar 11,636ft (3,500m) and the Adrar Zarzemt 10,213ft (3,100m). After an hour we reached Lake Tamda 8,750ft (2,600m) high and one of the most remote lakes in the entire High Atlas. Like Lake Ifni, Tamda does not encourage people to linger on its shores. The same eerie atmosphere surrounds it. The lake is dammed behind a massive build-up of what looks like moraine, but as the High Atlas does not have a glacial past I cannot imagine how this has happened. It is a strange place to find a lake.

From the lake, a steep descent leads down into an area of marsh land where the scenery broadens out into a wide valley with good grazing land and a few temporary shelters on the north side. Herds of goats were already grazing away on the land, even though the snows could not have long gone. The first sign of cultivation is reached near the point where the small river from Tamda is joined by the Assif Tichkiwine, and the track then continues down a narrow trail towards Tighza. We had been on the trail for nine hours by the time we arrived, exhausted, at Ighris. We found a place to stay almost immediately and borrowed boiling water to cook a couple of Remo's dehydrated mountain meals. He thought they were very good, but I could hardly eat them after the good fresh food we had been eating in the villages.

Since the master of the house could speak good French we talked into the night about the journeys he had made across the Atlas. Some of his epic trips made our little wanderings sound pathetic. There was scarcely a village in the High Atlas that he did not know and you could tell from the dignity of the man that he was not exaggerating. His journeys, like most travels by Berbers through their own mountains, were mostly in order to trade.

He had a gaslight attachment for a butane bottle which periodically flared up in a ball of flame because of a fault. When this happened he would laugh out loud, even though the flames were licking around the wooden ceiling. Then, with the room filled with the smell of gas, he would strike match after match to get it going again, still convulsed in laughter. This tendency to find disaster hilarious is a real trait of the Berbers. I suspect if you tied one to a railway track and told him the 10.47 express was due in two minutes, he would have killed himself laughing before the train arrived.

The seventh day of our hike was an easy haul along the road to Telouet, where the great Kasbah of the infamous Glaoui family can still be found. We wandered through the ornate, half-ruined rooms, savouring the atmosphere of the palace which has a bloody and turbulent history which only came to an end as recently as the 1950s. Gavin Maxwell's book *Lords of the Atlas* describes this period of Moroccan history extremely well, and it is required reading for anyone who wants to travel in the High Atlas. It is not a tale for the squeamish.

As we left the palace a coach of French tourists swept in. They looked shockingly clean and neat against our dusty and dirty appearance. They were the first foreigners we had seen since leaving the Ait Bou Guemez, one week before. Remo persuaded the tour leader to give us a lift back to Marrakesh. Seen through the windows of the air-conditioned bus, the mountains looked alien and unfamiliar. The spell of our journey was broken, and the cool beers of Marrakesh were waiting. The soothing voice of the tour leader began to describe how the Berbers live in the more remote mountain villages as I drifted into a fitful sleep.

Wheels over the Atlas
A Mountain Bike Trek to Zaouia Ahansal

I remember very clearly the first time I saw a mountain bike. It appeared on the front cover of the *Sunday Times*, New Year's Day, 1985. The photograph was taken on the summit of Kilimanjaro in east Africa. A caption informed readers that Nicholas and Richard Crane were the first to have made the climb with mountain bikes and that they had done so to raise money for the charity Intermediate Technology. The following years saw an explosion of interest in mountain bikes. Bike couriers used them to slalom at suicidal speed through grid-locked London traffic. Everything about these machines was fresh and new. They did to the standard conventional bicycle what the grey squirrel did for the red.

Cranky old gear systems were now replaced by state of the art technology, so that changing gear was smoother, quicker, and more precise. What was more, there were from 15–20 gears to choose from. The saddles were firm and ergonomic. The handgrips felt chunky and solid. The knobbly tyres gripped any surface better than the old version. You could jump the bike over or crash down pot holes and still feel comfortable. Equally impressive, the upright riding position gave a better view ahead in traffic. The designs became rapidly more outrageous and the colour schemes followed suit. People who had never shown any interest in bicycles now went out and bought a mountain bike.

Watching the mountain bike revolution in London I kept wondering what the real potential of these machines would be in the mountains. Many people seemed to be taking them up into the mountains of Wales and Scotland for the occasional day, while others were using them as long-haul overland transport for trips to India and the Far East. But nobody seemed to be trying long journeys which traversed entire mountain ranges. I found myself checking the terrain each time I went walking, trying to gauge if you could ride on it. The possibilities were intriguing. The principle factor which always limits what you can do in the mountains is time. Most people have very little enough time to spare for walking, and by the time you have added financial constraints, three to four weeks is usually the maximum. As a result the potential ground that can be covered is limited and most walks are measurable in tens of miles, rather than hundreds. Specific regions and areas can be explored in this way but entire ranges are out of the question. One of my ambitions had always been to make a traverse of the High Atlas range but time constraints had so far ruled it out.

The mountain bike opened up new options. Instead of travelling 20 miles (32km) a day on foot, it might be possible to cover 40–60 miles (60–100km) on bike. In this way, a three-week hike could cover an enormous distance. Parts of a mountain range which would never otherwise be visited could be traversed and experienced within the tight time and financial constraints of an annual holiday. The more I thought about

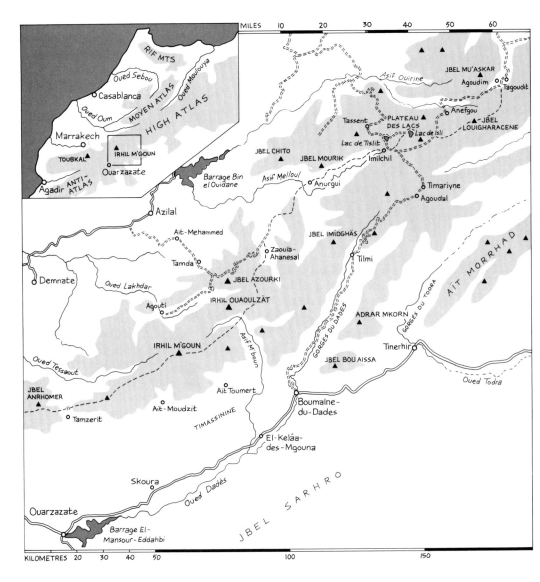

it, the more attractive the idea became. The only prospect that did not appeal was the certainty that, for long periods of ascent, the bike would have to be carried. Still, the exhilaration of the descents would compensate – would they not?

While thinking out these ideas, I began working on a new television series for Central TV and National Geographic Television. Called *Voyager* it consisted of 13 half-hour documentaries concentrating on travel, adventure and exploration. At a time when mountain biking was so popular, it clearly seemed opportune to launch a mountain bike adventure for the series. The most recent exciting developments in adventure film making seemed to have concentrated on hang-gliding and microlighting, and there was a strong need for something new. No one had yet made a documentary about a mountain bike journey. If we moved fast, ours would be the first. The trip would have to be difficult and visually spectacular. It would have to be practical to film and cheap enough to be filmed within a three-week period. The main question was, who would do the journey? The more we looked at this thorny problem, the more one name kept cropping up – Nick Crane. Not only did Nick have the reputation for tackling and completing extremely difficult journeys, he also possessed the journalistic skills which could elevate the film from the level of mere travelogue. The memory of that photograph on the front page of the *Sunday Times* was enough to make up our minds. The order came down from the chief executive of the series, 'Find Nick Crane'.

He was an elusive man to track down. One rumour suggested he was in Afghanistan on an aid mission to assist war victims, another whisper had him climbing down a volcano somewhere in Zaire. It turned out that the former was correct, and that he would shortly be returning to London. We finally found him in a room above a back-alley pub in the city. There was a meeting of an obscure travellers' club where returning wanderers met at irregular intervals to show slides and swap stories. Nick was looking thin and rather grey after a testing time in Afghanistan. The room was filled with the acrid smell of burning sausages. A blonde man who seemed to be a trainee Red Indian was demonstrating how to light a fire with a twig and grass. When we asked Nick if he would like to get involved in a mountain bike film he looked around the crowded room and took a sip of Guinness before replying, 'Sounds like a good idea. I could do with a holiday.' It was on.

First we had to work out which journey would fit the brief. We sat down with Nick and began to thrash out the possibilities. Turkey was possible. The Pyrenees? The Ruwenzoris? The higher the cost of getting the crew out there, the less time we would be able to afford on location. How about Scandinavia? Or Russia? Then we began looking seriously at the High Atlas. Nick knew them from a previous trip, and so did I.

We reckoned the high-altitude mule tracks would be perfect for mountain biking. In three weeks it might just be possible to traverse the whole range. Together with Chris Bradley, who had been involved with the project from the beginning, we calculated likely daily distances on the tracks, then worked on daily averages for the sections where we knew he would have to carry the bike.

But there was still something missing. Whilst the idea of traversing the High Atlas was good and sound, there was no real beginning or end. We could pick excellent starting and finishing points but none really seemed better than the rest. It was Nick who solved the problem by realizing that we should extend the journey so that it ran from the fringes of the Sahara to the sea. This became the project name and it gave the ride a good deal more diversity. We could pack in the great sand sea at Merzouga and have a grand finale at the beach at Agadir. This journey also added several hundred additional miles to the ride, but we would just have to increase our daily averages in the mountains to compensate. By stretching pieces of string across the map, we estimated the total to be covered was about 620 miles (1,000km).

After getting the green light from National Geographic in America, we started the logistical exercise of putting the show on the road. First came the bikes which Nick obtained, and then an enormous number of spares and other equipment. The bikes were the latest 'Ridgeback' models, sprayed in yellow and black paint. Next came the vehicles in the form of two long-wheelbase Landrovers. One was equipped with a roof-rack. The film crew and their equipment, was the next consideration. Few people who watch a television programme have any idea of the massive amount of gear that is involved. The programme would be made on 16mm film. Once the camera bodies, range of lenses, batteries, film stock, tripods and sound gear is assembled in flight cases, it weighs in at several

Leaving the Erg Chebbi at the beginning of the trans-High Atlas mountain bike traverse. (Photograph by Andy Flanders.)

hundred kilos. The crew would consist of the director, cameraman, camera assistant, and sound man. The other members of the expedition were a mechanic, a cook, a Moroccan translator and an additional Moroccan driver. Television production is an expensive business.

By the time we gathered for the start of the journey at the top of the highest sand dune in Morocco, it already felt as though we had undertaken a major trip. We assembled the bikes and pedalled off on the first section of the journey. This would be quite straightforward using the tarmac roads through Rissani, Erfoud, Er Rachidia and Rich. There we would leave the tarmac behind and take to the 'piste' to Imilchil. It took us four days to travel 223 miles (360km), crossing the Tizi-n-Firest and Tizi-n-Ali on the way, enjoying the beautiful flower-filled valley of the Gorges du Ziz. The bikes performed extremely well and we were on schedule as we rode into the mountain village of Imilchil

just before sunset. This is the scene of a festival each September where Berber tribes from the surrounding area bring their young men and women for matchmaking and marriage. It is a joyful event, filled with colour and dance, and is evidence, if any is needed, that the tribes of the Atlas are alive and well.

At Imilchil the expedition completely changed. The real test was about to begin. It was the moment Chris, Nick and I had been looking forward to for months, the moment when we would leave behind the vehicles and roads and go onto the mule tracks alone. We would be taking an Aaton 16mm camera with us to cover the significant moments. The rest of the crew would descend on the road to the north and then regain height with a climb up a jeep track to Zaouia Ahansal where we would all rendezvous. The last sequence filmed showed the three of us looking at the prospects ahead on the only map of the area we had. It was an atrocious map, a free hand-out from a French guide to the central Atlas. There were red blobs, yellow blobs and dotted lines. None of them could have been translated by even the most optimistic cartographer into information that could be useful to prospective mountain travellers. The only certainty was that somewhere away to the south-west was a destination called Zaouia Ahansal. We were about to find out if mountain bikes were good news in the Atlas.

Our departure was filled with expectation and high hopes. We left late in the day with just enough light to ride for one hour at most. It would have been far more sensible to stay in Imilchil that night and start afresh in the morning, but our itinerary was so tight that not an hour could be wasted. We rode the trail to the village of Oudeddi. The setting sun vanished behind the skyline of the surrounding ridges as the bikes whirred along effortlessly in top gear down the slight incline. It was true to say that we really had no idea how long this stage to Ahansal would take. Whatever happened, we would be totally dependent on finding food in the passing villages since we had nothing but a couple of chocolate bars each.

The few villagers on the path waved and smiled enthusiastically as we passed. There were two women carrying bundles of animal fodder, a boy with a couple of fat sheep in his charge, and a man who shouted in French 'Where are you going?' 'Zaouia Ahansal!' we replied. He shook his head and pointed the other way. 'But that's where the road is. We're taking the mountain tracks!' Before he had time to reply we were gone. All three of us knew that the sensible route was the one taken by the vehicles but that was a boring approach. We had set ourselves the objective of an east to west traverse, and that was what we were going to do.

At the village we rode up through narrow passages to a dusty square, flanked by a mosque. Our arrival had not gone unnoticed. Faces peeped from doorways, and children leant

A woman collects animal fodder, High Atlas Mountains.

around the mud walls of the mosque to get a better look. The sight of three rather dusty and brightly clad mountain bikers is obviously not an everyday occurrence in the village of Oudeddi. High up on the cliffs above the wadi, goatherds were lighting fires. This caused almost as much of a stir as had our arrival, prompting small groups of women to emerge from the solidly built houses to watch the spectacle. Strangely, there seemed to be no men. Nick went on a circuit of the village to find an old building or outhouse we could sleep in for the night. Meanwhile children became bolder and, responding to our smiles, gathered around the bicycles in an excited group. We mimed 'sleep' but this only provoked a fresh bout of giggling. The women kept a discreet distance, clearly wary of these three strangers. Then Nick returned with good news. A young man by the name of Saïd Amgoul had offered us his granary for the night. The room was warm and dry, with lumpy

33

The madder side of mountain biking. (Photograph by Nick Crane.)

hessian sacks piled up at one end and domestic bits and pieces at the other. Next to our home for the night was a narrow corridor. It was pitch black and we were startled, as we moved through it, to sense an animal breathing next to us. It sounded big. Chris flashed a torch and the culprit, a young bullock, shuffled back in alarm. 'Breakfast', Chris joked.

Saïd returned with a gas-powered lamp and led us into the family room where his mother, father and sister were waiting to greet us. A stove fashioned from a 50-gallon oil drum was pumping out a wall of welcoming heat. Saïd's sister began spinning wool as we explained to the two men in a mixture of French and Arabic what we were up to. They were fascinated by the route that had brought us here. The father, Hassan, was good on his Moroccan geography

and took great pleasure from reciting, in order, the oasis towns we had passed through from Merzouga. But when we told them our destination, the mood changed. Both our hosts agreed that we were attempting an extremely difficult route. There would be two villages to pass and a lot of climbing. Saïd signified this by crooking his leg at an acute angle and walking two fingers up it with much melodramatic huffing and puffing. Why, they asked, didn't we take the road?

Several hours later Saïd's mother produced a steaming 'tagine' clay pot. It was filled with a rich collection of carrots, potatoes, and onions. We ate by dipping warm bread into the stew and lifting it out with as many vegetables as was possible to balance on top. Hassan was a gracious and generous host, picking out pieces of choice vegetable or gristly meat and placing them firmly on our plates. Compared to the previous meals which we had shared with the support crew, this was eating in style. Nick had a complimentary phrase for it, 'stodge factor' because cyclists need 'stodge' in abundant quantities, and the bread and potato of that Berber meal was ideal. We thanked our hosts by giving them a gift of money so they could replenish their supplies. A village like Oudeddi has few enough food resources without mountain bikers eating into them.

The next day began optimistically. Saïd guided us out to the track which would lead deep into the heart of the central High Atlas. A thin layer of ground frost carpeted the shaded part of the route and we wore hats and a thermal layer to combat the penetrating cold. Morocco is commonly perceived to be a warm country but the High Atlas in January can be as bitter as anything experienced in a European winter.

The warm-up period for a cyclist is much longer than for a walker. The legs heat-up quickly, but the upper torso, deprived of any significant movement, remains painfully cold for quite a while. The hands are even more prone to wind chill, and we often found that our down gloves were not enough. The face takes a battering too, with cold air hammering it at four or five times the rate the walker experiences, the wind chill factor again causing problems. Sunburn strikes quicker in these circumstances, so Chris and I took great care to use plenty of high-factor cream. Nick preferred to rely on his trilby hat!

The track followed the Asif Melloul river, cut deep into a gorge. Caught up in the enthusiasm of the ride we managed to steer ourselves into a dead-end valley where we lost valuable time fighting through a thicket of thorn bushes before realizing our mistake and turning back. This was another difference between the biker and the walker. The biker keeps his eyes permanently down on the track watching for a stone or rock. The walker can afford the luxury of admiring the scenery while his legs go on autopilot.

The riding continued, in the lowest of our 21 gears, up a steeper incline towards the village of Oulghazi. This was more difficult terrain for cycling, with fragmented rocks disrupting progress and snagging at the pedals on each downward stroke. A persistent ache attacked both my knees on this uphill struggle as we puffed and panted up the slope. Chris went down to speak to the villagers as Nick and I carried on up the path which skirted the flank of a large bend in the valley. It seemed to be heading directly for a cliff face. Chris came back with unwelcome news: 'Eight hours walking to a place called Anurgui, and then at least another day's walking to Zaouia Ahansal.' How reliable those estimates were was unknown, but with our tight schedule it now became even more critical that we made fast progress. The crunch question was, how much of the route could we ride?

At the foot of the cliff, for the first time since leaving Merzouga hundreds of miles before, we began to carry the bikes. We used various techniques. Chris adopted the classic style, resting the crossbar over his shoulder. Nick and I went for the technique discovered by Nick's cousin during a 14-peaks attempt in Wales several years earlier. This involved putting head and shoulders through the main frame triangle so that the down-tube of the bike rested square across the shoulders. But whatever technique you use, there is one inescapable fact — mountain bikes are heavy. And with the weight of the panniers they are extremely heavy. Since the sun was now high in the sky, we shed several layers of clothing as the climb continued. Sweat continually ran into my eyes and dripped uncomfortably down my back. Three hours later we gained the top of the gorge. The view was spectacular to the south, with snow-capped peaks emerging from the heat haze. There, 2,000ft (609m) below us, the Asif Melloul ran south-west, the direction we knew would take us

The climb up from Oulghazi, High Atlas Mountains. (Photograph by Nick Crane.)

to Zaouia Ahansal. The scene was reminiscent of the Grand Canyon. Nick went down with his bike to a slab of rock that jutted out into the gorge and we took some photographs.

The view put us into a good frame of mind but, although we had not voiced it, our fears were growing. So far that day we had worked hard to make progress. A couple of filming stops had cost us time. The gorge wall had cost us the best part of half a day, with no horizontal gain made on the distance to Ahansal. Carrying the bikes was slow and painful. Nick calculated that at our current rate it could take us five days to reach Ahansal. If it did, our plan would be over. We would have to leave the high-altitude mule tracks and ride the jeep tracks and roads that flanked the range at lesser heights. The villages would be less interesting, the challenge would be negligible, and the film would be a flop. The consequences did not bear thinking about. We

leaped on the bikes and pedalled furiously across the col. There was not a moment to be lost.

As was often the case Chris was leading as we swept down the steep, dusty trail that plummeted from the col. His background as a competitive cyclo-cross rider gave him an advantage, as did the fact that he was lighter and more agile than Nick and I. But as we steered the Ridgebacks along the hairpin trail I saw Chris crash in spectacular fashion. One moment he was there, the next he was gone in a flurry of dust and bicycle bits. When Nick and I raced to the scene it was clear that Chris was badly hurt. He sat, crumpled up in pain, swearing and moaning. The fall had sent him right over the handlebars. His knee had taken the entire impact as his body hit the rocks. The wound was slight, little more than a graze. Yet from the swelling of the knee joint there was obviously internal damage.

Chris just moments after his accident. (Photograph by Nick Crane.)

For the sake of the documentary, I assembled the camera equipment and filmed Chris being treated by Nick. In reality there was little we could do except bathe the knee and clean out the wound. Now we really had a problem. Zaouia Ahansal was a good two days' trekking away and Chris was not going to be fit enough to ride. We discussed the possibility of returning to Imilchil but there was little that could be done there for Chris. Besides, the film crew would already be waiting for us in Ahansal.

It took Chris an hour to recover from the nausea and dizziness caused by the accident. Then we decided to search for somewhere to spend the night since it was getting close to sunset. Gritting his teeth Chris stumbled bravely on, while Nick and I pondered the best course of action. Luckily, before dark, we did find an isolated hamlet of three Berber homes. The families understood our predicament as soon as they saw Chris's knee and they were kind

enough to let us sleep on a floor. Chris sat for the whole evening in a state of dejection. His knee was swollen to the size of a football and he could bend it only with great difficulty. Even the magnificent plate of couscous that our hosts provided could not dislodge the thought that Chris may have to abandon the ride. It would be a cruel blow after so many months of hard training.

When morning came Chris's knee was still swollen and stiff. We considered the possibility that he should wait at the hamlet while Nick and I went to get help. But, despite the pain, Chris preferred to continue to Ahansal. Much against Chris's will, Nick and I split some of his gear between us, but he would still have to carry his bike – not even Nick volunteered to carry two bikes across the High Atlas!

After a warming breakfast of freshly baked bread and olive oil, we left with our host, Mohammed, as guide. He took us to the edge of

37

Day 6 of the mountain bike journey – Chris and Nick approaching Anurgui village.

a great ravine and pointed vaguely in the general direction of the other side. That, he assured us, was the route for Anurgui. The descent was through a woodland of noble pine trees, the last of the millions which had once forested the High Atlas. Every year thousands more are cut down for firewood, and the problems of soil erosion become more pressing. At the bottom of the chasm was a sandy wadi which we followed north for a short while before climbing again to the west. The path was ill-defined and difficult to trace. Sometimes it split in a fork. Which to choose? Left or right? Nick's compass was our only means of deciding, the map was completely useless. By late morning we were lost again. A shepherd pointed us back in the right direction, further to the south-west, along a dry river bed which angled sharply up a dramatically eroded gully. Manhandling the bikes up the sheer faces of the falls was difficult due to a layer of transparent ice which made every footstep treacherous. Chris was finding it

extremely difficult. At lunchtime we stopped and nibbled the chocolate.

At last we emerged from the never-ending gully after a two-hour climb. Our reward was being surrounded by a pack of dogs which appeared from nowhere and then vanished back to wherever they came from once they saw the size of the rocks with which we threatened them. It was getting colder by the minute as we climbed first one, then another false summit. Where was the top? We were supposed to be keeping an appointment in Zaouia Ahansal about now, but we were not even halfway there.

We hit the snow line at 8,530ft (2,600m) and half an hour later reached the top of the pass. Chris looked yellow, and was trying to suppress the pain. I could see by the way he put down the bike it was a relief for him to stand still for a moment. And then the wind began to bite. This pass was too exposed to rest on, tired as we were. Nick consulted the compass once again and we followed a pencil-thin track to the edge. I grabbed a handful of snow to eat as we looked at the options. It was a simple choice. We could stay high and try to follow a ridge line which manifestly went the wrong way. Or we could descend a ferociously steep escarpment to what might or might not be the valley in which the elusive town of Anurgui was hidden. At least that was the right direction. Just.

We went down. It was a helter-skelter fall of about 4,921ft (1,500m). Nick went first, a blazing trail of zigzagging dust spewing out behind his wheels. After the long hours of carrying bikes we were revelling in the chance to ride them again. In the exhilaration of the moment, we forgot the risks. I went next with my heart in my mouth. The speed was intoxicating. The 'zigs' were manageable. It was the 'zags' that caused the adrenalin rush. They were the hairpin bends at the end of each straight section of track. At these points the track seemed to fall abruptly away into thin air. The best technique was to approach the bend as fast as possible, then slam on the rear brake slewing the back wheel in a 180° arc, kicking up stones like shrapnel.

When it worked it was fine. The bike would flow around the 'zag' like a snake unravelling a coil. When it did not, the rider would be unbalanced and would be dumped on the wrong side of the bend in a heap. I saw it happen a couple of times to Nick, and fell victim to it myself four or five times. On each occasion I escaped without injury. Once or twice, though, a nagging strain in my knee threatened to snap as I went one way and the bike went another. Wisely, Chris walked. Halfway down I caught up with Nick. He was flushed with the excitement of the ride. 'This is pretty marginal stuff' he yelled, slewing round another crook in the track with an elegant shift of balance in the saddle. Within half an hour we had reached the bottom of the valley. Chris arrived not long after, and we all rode the last stretch down to Anurgui.

Consistent with our run of bad luck the village market was closed. Only a deserted compound greeted our hungry eyes. A feral dog rooted for bones in a rubbish pile, and the shell of a long-abandoned Landrover lay by the mosque. It felt as though the entire town had taken a holiday a long way away. No one had noticed our arrival. Eventually we did find a run-down shop in which an old man sat cross-legged amongst his goods. He sold us sardines and condensed milk. It was not an inspiring feast, but we gobbled up the food nevertheless.

This stop gave us another opportunity to change our route. Anurgui was linked to the outside world by a jeep track. By heading north on this 'piste' we could have cycled all the way to Zaouia Ahansal although this would have represented a massive detour of more than 93 miles (150km). The decision rested with Chris and he bravely decided that we should stick to the direct high-level route. Our destination could not be that much further, could it?

For the next 2½ miles we rode along a delightful trail. The river lay below us and on the flat flood plain of the valley were groves of walnut trees and fields of potatoes and mint. Everybody seemed to be outside, enjoying the late afternoon sun. As we flashed past on the bikes they shouted out 'Where are you going?' We yelled back 'Ahansal', and of course, as we had by now come to expect, they pointed back in the direction we had just come from. There was much shouting and giving of advice, and they all agreed that theoretically it was possible to go by the direct route. They just could not understand why we were going to do it when the track was so much better.

It was not long before the track became too steep to ride. Unlike the Oulghazi region where the rock was frost shattered and heavily eroded by water action, the cliffs that faced us were solid and intact. The walls fell for many hundreds of metres. The geological structure of the rock had produced a heavily striated effect which made it look in cross-section as if a new layer of molten rock had been poured on each year and left to set, rather as icing is spread on top of a cake. The colours were accentuated by the low light of the setting sun. Reds and ochres, browns and blacks, all in orderly lines along the sculpted rock and here and there we could see sturdy pines growing straight from the rock on some impossibly narrow ledge.

Cut into the softer bands of rock was a path which traversed the cliff face. It took us to a concealed opening which led to the plateau top. We walked across it on a well-defined path as the sun set on day three of our departure from Imilchil. It was a cloudless night, and a rapier-like wind began to blow an icy chill which froze the sweat on our bodies from the hard climb up. A man with his wife perched on a mule quickly passed by. He said there were woodcutters' cottages one hour away. When we arrived there, we shouted greetings from outside, but no one emerged to ask who we were. If you have to arrive unannounced it is always better to do so

The cameraman sits on the Landrover to get the shot he needs.

before dark. Now, since the only welcome was the baying of guard dogs we moved on into the night, cold, hungry, and facing a night out in our bivvy bags. Chris was getting slower by the minute.

The moon rose, casting a clinical white light on the scene and the patches of snow became more frequent. We had run out of water some four hours before. Now, with no prospect of finding more supplies on the plateau, a few mouthfuls of compacted snow was the best we could hope for to alleviate our thirst. But to our great surprise we did stumble across a deep well. Torchlight revealed that it was heavily polluted with animal droppings, and covered with a thick layer of frozen brown scum. We were thirsty, but not that thirsty.

Nick was keen to press on through the night but Chris and I thought our chances of getting lost were too great. We had already lost valuable time hunting for the right route, and the

thought of doing it again was not attractive. We found a well-protected site beneath the maternal spread of an ancient tree and climbed into our bags. We carefully shared out the last chocolate bar and an orange. Without foam mats, the frozen ground stole precious heat away from our inert bodies. Even the foil survival bags around the sleeping bags did not seem capable of keeping us warm. The night passed in that fitful, unsatisfying state of sleep when the cold seeps into the bones, and the slightest movement sacrifices hard-won warmth.

With me in the sack was my water bottle packed with as much snow as I could cram into it. Chris and Nick were sceptical about this attempt to create drinking water and laughed at my obvious discomfort as I placed the bottle next to the warmest part of the body, the groin. It was excruciatingly uncomfortable but by 3 a.m. I was rewarded with about a third of a pint of meltwater. It certainly helped alleviate my thirst, because we were all seriously dehydrated after our 18-hour day. Had there been gallons there I could have drunk them.

We woke next morning to find that we were covered with a thick layer of groundfrost. There was no breakfast to delay us so we packed, did some filming, and left. The morning passed in an agony of carrying, and while the path was not difficult to follow it was virtually unrideable. Beyond, the plateau was vast. Every way we looked it stretched to the horizon, featureless and bleak. Every half-hour we might come to a short stretch which could be ridden. We leaped on the bikes only stopping when the size and placement of the rocks meant that more progress was impossible. These were the high-level mule tracks we were supposed to be riding at 10 miles (16km) per hour. In reality, weighed down by the bikes, we were doing less than a third this speed.

Where was Zaouia Ahansal? It was beginning to be more than a joke. We were getting seriously annoyed with the place. Shepherds on the plateau confirmed we were on the right track.

Crossing the Tizi-n-Timilit, High Atlas Mountains. (Photograph by Nick Crane.)

At 7 a.m. one told us it was two hours away. At 11 a.m. we were told it was three hours away. By midday another informant placed it one hour away. At 4 p.m., yet another shepherd put it at five hours away. Chris exploded, 'These people haven't got the foggiest idea where the ***** place is!' The trouble was, neither did we.

The amusing little songs we had sung to keep up our spirits had subsided with our depressing situation. We were dying to stop and rest but, with no food and water, there was little point, and of course Chris was still hobbling at the back. At last we came to a collection of houses nestled into a scenic valley which looked more like Greece than Morocco. A woman gave us eggs and tea. It was a charming pause in an otherwise horrendous day. 'How far to Zaouia Ahansal?' we asked. 'Two hours . . . just down there' was the reply. It really was unbelievable. No matter how hard we tried we never seemed to get any nearer.

As the afternoon wore on we were each filled with the dread that we might not get there that night. This became a serious possibility when we came to the edge of a truly phenomenal cliff. The path that went down it was the steepest imaginable without the need for ropes. We used the last few feet of camera film, and began the descent. At the bottom of the cliff came a tiring further descent down a path which was obstructed by an unusually high number of fallen trees. Then, finally and magically, just as it was getting dark, we reached a jeep track. Chris was looking like death. The descents were particularly grating on his still swollen knee. A new mood of elation swept over us. Surely our destination must be just around the corner? We set off in high spirits. It grew dark. We pedalled on with no lights, but with the moon hiding behind the clouds we had to slow right down. And the track simply went on and on for ever. Behind me I could hear Chris swearing and cursing from the pain. Nick had gone ahead, looking grey and tired.

41

The first winter ascent of Mount Toubkal with mountain bikes.

Mountain bike descent of Mount Toubkal, Morocco. (Photograph by Annabel Huxley.)

I felt completely sapped of all energy. We no longer believed that we would ever find this mythical place. A dog rushed out and snapped at my heels. I shouted at it so savagely that it dropped back. I think it could tell that I was in no mood for play. Then at long last, hours into the night, when every last muscle was ready to give up, a string of lights appeared ahead. Hardly daring to believe that it was anything other than a figment of my fatigued imagination, I saw the Landrovers parked next to a roaring fire. There was only one thought on my mind – to eat and drink. Anything would do, just so long as it was not sardines and condensed milk. I swept down the path and was greeted by the film crew and Nick. 'Is this it?' I asked, 'Is this *really* Zaouia Ahansal?' Alan Ravenscroft, the director, answered: 'Well, almost – the actual town is just up there . . .'

In the post-mortem that followed we digested a few home truths. Was it possible to move quickly through the wilder parts of the High Atlas using mountain bikes on high-altitude mule tracks? The answer was unequivocably No. We had been prepared for a high percentage of carrying. Even 50 per cent would have been acceptable if we had been able to ride quickly for the rest of the time. But in fact we had carried the bikes for at least 90 per cent of the route. In sheer logistical terms it had been a disaster. We had severely underestimated the problems. Chris had suffered a nasty accident (which forced him to back out), and we had often gone hungry and thirsty.

Crossing a wadi at Rich in the Eastern High Atlas. The film crew are in foreground.

In front of us now was at least another 372 miles (600km) but fortunately a good deal of it would be on jeep tracks where we could definitely ride. In fact we never encountered any conditions which matched the sheer, gruelling hardship of that Imilchil to Ahansal section. Furthermore, we had accurate maps for the rest of the trip.

Human nature is perverse. Imilchil to Ahansal had been a disaster yet, when I think back on the entire expedition, it is the one section that stands out above the rest. Perhaps it was because it was a journey without maps. Perhaps it was the hospitality we experienced from villagers who hardly ever see a traveller. Perhaps it had been the grandeur of the scenery, the cliffs, and the plateau. Perhaps it was because during those days we experienced a rare chance to have something called an adventure. I just do not know, but whatever it was, it was fun.

At least now, as the brightly clad warriors flash by in the streets of London with their Day-Glo mountain bikes, I know what the machines can do. It was not the limitations of the bikes which let us down, it was the fact that mountain bikes and mule tracks do not mix. So if you find yourself thinking about Imilchil to Zaouia Ahansal, do what is best throughout the High Atlas and travel by foot. Take my advice and do not, I repeat, do not, take a mountain bike!

The Toubkal Circuit

The Toubkal circuit is one of the most popular treks in North Africa. Its ease of access from the nearby towns of Marrakesh, Agadir and Casablanca has stimulated a constant influx of trekkers and climbers since the Moroccan tourist industry began its expansion in the early 1970s. The region is dotted with huts built by the CAF (Club Alpin Français), and accommodation in Berber villages is widely available. Unusually for most mountain ranges in Africa, the Toubkal region is well served by maps and there are usually excellent mountain guides to be hired from the basecamp villages. For those who are reluctant to carry their own pack, mules are available at reasonable rates.

According to Pearce and Smith's *World Weather Guide* the highest temperature ever recorded in Marrakesh was 120°F (49°C). Summer on the Moroccan plains is not for the fainthearted. Yet, just a short distance to the south, the High Atlas enjoy a much more temperate climate where hiking is possible throughout the summer, even though the range lies geographically at the northern edge of the Sahara desert.

Despite its geographical location on the 'doorstep' of Europe, Morocco remained virtually unknown to outsiders right up to the beginning of the twentieth century. Gavin Maxwell wrote of Morocco, in his classic book *Lords of the Atlas* that it was 'as unknown as Tibet, xenophobe and mysterious, guarding splendours and horrors that the wildest travellers tales could not exaggerate'. The only way an 'infidel' could penetrate the veil of secrecy that shrouded Morocco was in disguise. In 1883 Père Charles de Foucauld disguised himself as a Jewish trader and made a long and perilous journey deep into the Atlas. He crossed the Tizi-n-Telouet and explored some of the previously unknown oasis towns of the south. On many occasions he came close to being discovered, a fate which would have meant certain death. One chief wished to hold him for ransom; on another occasion a rumour spread that he was a Christian laden with gold. Each time he was lucky to escape.

Another great early explorer of the High Atlas was the Englishman Walter B Harris. In 1893 he crossed the High Atlas to the oasis towns of the Tafilet. His book *Tafilate. The narrative of a journey of exploration in the Atlas Mountains and of the Oases of the north-west Sahara* was published in 1895 and it remains a classic work on the region. The most fascinating part of the narrative is the section where Harris describes in detail the expedition of the Sultan Mulai el Hassen whose party consisted of more than 40,000 followers and 10,000 pack animals. But there was a dark side to these wild Atlas tribes as Harris records: 'The slave trade flourishes at Tafilet, the slaves being brought direct to that spot from the Sudan. At the time of my visit they were being freely hawked about the Sultan's camp. The girls of the Hausa country fetched the best prices, being considered

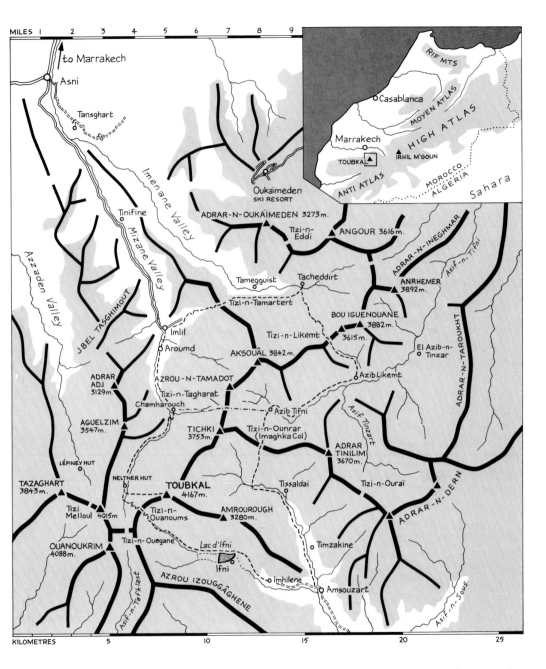

to Marrakech

Asni

Tansghart

RIF MTS

Casablanca

MOYEN ATLAS

Marrakech

HIGH ATLAS

TOUBKAL △ △ IRHIL M'GOUN

ANTI ATLAS

MOROCCO
ALGERIA   Sahara

Imenane Valley

Tinifine

Mizane Valley

Oukaïmeden
SKI RESORT

ADRAR-N-OUKAÏMEDEN 3273m.

Tizi-n-
Eddi

ANGOUR 3616m. ▲

ADRAR-N-INEGHMAR

Asif-n-Tifni

Azzaden Valley

JBEL TASGHIMOUT

Tamegguist

Tacheddirt

ANRHEMER
3892m. ▲

Tizi-n-Tamartert

BOU IGUENOUANE
3882m. ▲

Imlil

Aroumd

Tizi-n-Likemt

3615m.

El Azib-n-
Tinzar

ADRAR-N-TAROUKHT

AKSOUÂL 3842m. ▲

ADRAR
ADJ
3129m. ▲

AZROU-N-TAMADOT

Tizi-n-Tagharat

Azib Likemt

Chamharouch

Azib Tifni

AGUELZIM
3547m. ▲

TICHKI
3753m. ▲

Tizi-n-Ounrar
(Imaghka Col)

Asif Tinzart

ADRAR
TINILIM
3670m. ▲

LÉPINEY HUT

NELTNER HUT

TAZAGHART
3843m. ▲

TOUBKAL
4167m.

Tissaldai

Tizi-n-Ouraï

ADRAR-N-DERN

Tizi
Melloul 4015m

Tizi-n-
Ouanoums

AMROUROUGH
3280m. ▲

OUANOUKRIM
4088m. ▲

Tizi-n-Ouagane

Lac d'Ifni

Timzakine

Asif-n-Sous

Asif-n-Tafklast

Ifni

AZROU IZOUGGÂGHENE

Imhilene

Amsouzart

more cheerful and neater than those from far-ther west.' Less than 100 years later, the country that was once one of the most secretive and in-accessible in the world is now host to millions of tourists. I wonder what Walter Harris would have made of the billboard posters in the

London Underground which advertise the delights of Morocco? Amongst the collage of photographs on the poster is a woman in a skimpy bikini, and a close-up of a woman in a veil.

The French colonial period saw a growth of interest in the High Atlas which resulted in the

45

first realization of its potential for climbing and trekking. Amongst the early climbers credited with first ascents were Louis Neltner and J and T de Lepiney. Their names live on, honouring the huts of the CAF in the Toubkal.

The literature on the area and its people is mostly French, but there are some good exceptions. One of the most useful is Bryan Clarke's book *Berber Village*, which describes an Oxford University expedition to the High Atlas in 1955. The objective was to study the people, fauna and flora of the range. Although much of the information contained is now obviously out of date, the book remains a remarkably accurate portrait of life in the High Atlas. Many of the insights into village life are as relevant now as they were in 1955. (Although the book is now out of print copies are sometimes available in libraries and specialist booksellers. It is well worth tracking down a copy.)

Throughout the 1960s the walking potential of the High Atlas continued to be developed. The visitors were then mostly French, although others come from Britain, Italy, Spain and Switzerland. By the 1970s however, the High Atlas was well and truly established as a viable and exotic alternative to a season in the Alps or Pyrenees. Ski mountaineering became increasingly common, although by far the majority of visitors came to the region to walk. It was close to Europe, cheap, and offered exciting scenery. But most importantly, it was a chance to experience the culture of the Berber people.

The next, inevitable development came with the arrival of commercial walking tours in the area. By the mid-1980s, there were British, French and Italian walking companies operating regular seasons in the High Atlas. The Berber villagers gain financially by hiring out mules, acting as guides, and providing accommodation. But the longer term, less desirable effect is worrying. Will the High Atlas villages

Lunch break for trekking group in High Atlas.

be ruined by such concentrated numbers of hikers? How will their traditional life be changed?

I was very conscious of these possible dangers when I accepted a job from a British adventure company. They had recognized the potential of the High Atlas and, knowing my experience in the area, asked if I would set up their first season's trekking programme. The prospect of a summer in the High Atlas was too enticing to turn down. I flew out to Marrakesh and began the preparations just one week before the first group arrived. The initial task was to head up into the mountains to find a reliable guide with whom I could work for the summer. Not only would he have to be head man and 'fixer' of accommodation in the villages, but he would have to run the team of muleteers too. The one name that kept cropping up was Brahim Ait El Kadi. He could be found at Aroumd and had a good reputation for working with foreign groups. I set off from Marrakesh on the normal Asni to Imlil route to find him. At Imlil I let it be known I was looking for a guide for the summer. There were some excellent candidates but Brahim, once I had tracked him down, did seem the best. A small man with a slight limp, he had spent much of his life guiding groups and was enthusiastic about the coming season.

We travelled up the valley to Aroumd, a village perched on a curious outspur of rock which cuts across the Mizane valley at an unlikely angle. Brahim's three-storey house, was situated in the shade of huge walnut trees. At the bottom was a kitchen and storeroom; one layer up was a sleeping room and further storage space; and at the top, in the tradition of the Berber villages, was a communal guest room. The structure also included a stabling area for livestock, and a loft in which rabbits and chickens ran free. A terrace connected to the communal room.

On the terrace a mat was laid down and we sat cross-legged to discuss the prices for the season.

Berbers are superb negotiators and Brahim was a well-practised master of the art. On my side, however, was the considerable bargaining stance of being able to offer a whole season's work. When tea arrived Brahim carefully filled the pot with fresh mint and sugar before pouring it out into dainty cups. We reached a final agreement later that day on the prices for guiding and mules. Individual arrangements with villagers for food and accommodation would have to be made *en route*, but Brahim promised to help with these negotiations.

I returned to Marrakesh to meet my first group, feeling rather nervous about the enterprise. What would they be like? Would they be super-fit athletes or conked out wrecks? Most important of all, how would they fare in the mountains. When they arrived most of my fears were immediately laid to rest. They seemed a sensible and well-travelled group. Most had had good trekking experience in Britain and Europe, some had an enormous range of mountain history behind them, and those were veterans of the Himalayas and Andes. We spent just one day in Marrakesh to get final supplies and then left in a convoy of shared taxis for the mountains.

The route I had selected offered the best view of the High Atlas and could be comfortably tackled in one week. And since the entire group was keen to explore the villages on the way, there was no point in rushing ahead unnecessarily fast. The circuit began and ended at the village of Imlil or Aroumd, and entailed a loop around Toubkal enabling us to explore some villages on the southern slopes of the range. The paths were all well defined and mules could be utilized throughout the trip. In this way one could set off on the Toubkal circuit carrying nothing more than a day-pack with water, and personal items such as chocolate, camera, binoculars and wet-weather gear. As one of the group put it, 'Let the mule take the strain'.

After a few days' walking to acclimatize the

group and get them used to the local conditions, we set off. The first part of the journey follows the established path to the Neltner hut via Sidi Charamouch. From the hut is the prospect of a day's climb to the summit of Toubkal (*see* Trying Times on Toubkal for more details on the ascent), before the real circuit begins. Leaving Neltner the path strikes south up the valley, skirting the infrequent patches of flat grass which mark the highest springs of the river that feeds down into the Mizane. Then starts a deadly zigzag scree climb which is the tedious ascent to the Tizi Ouanoums. This tizi, or col, marks the end of the WSW ridge of Toubkal and is one of the three recognized routes out of the valley. The others are the Tizi-n-Ouagane at 12,253ft (3,730m) and the Tadat col at 12,270ft (3,740m).

The Tizi Ouanoums begins at 12,020ft (3,600m) and takes a good two hours from the Neltner hut which always looks infuriatingly nearby from wherever you are in the upper Mizane. The scree of the Ouanoums is rather in the style of the scree on Toubkal, a foul concoction of ankle-twisting rocks which conspire to rob thighs and calves of every ounce of energy. Stragglers at the end of the party fall victim to a powdery light dust which rises from the paths. The path itself is very steep and marked by the occasional cairn. Mules ascend this col only with the utmost persuasion from their guardians. On some occasions we had to unload them and carry their loads ourselves.

Once the col is reached the walker is rewarded by the first glimpse of Lake Ifni. This is a remarkable feature of the Toubkal region but is strangely reluctant to reveal itself from any of the significant nearby vantage points. It cannot be seen from the summit of Toubkal. And even from the top of the Tizi Ouanoums it only teases the eager spectator with a view of the corner. From high, the lake has an emerald green colour

The Berbers are great builders, their villages built up over centuries.

which contrasts abruptly with the lighter rock around. The descent to the lake is one of those knee-jarring affairs which linger long in the memory. The 4,265ft (1,300m) of continuous downward motion is enough to tax even the strongest legs. The Berber muleteers have an extraordinary technique for persuading their mules to go down. This involved running at the steeper zigzag falls at a speed which gave the poor beasts no time to think about their plight. At each corner the Berbers would tug the mule roughly round the bend and the rear quarters would follow suit. It looked dramatic and painfully dangerous but in all my time in the High Atlas I never saw a mule damaged by the practice or visibly upset.

The only good part of the descent is the everpresent High Atlas scree. All the heavily used passes have had their rocks pounded and crushed by generations of passers and, if you are prepared to take the risk, a fast descent is often possible. If you get it right, it can be an exhilarating experience. If you get it wrong, you end up running at full tilt into a jumble of unyielding rocks which will quite easily break a leg. At the bottom of the wall the path follows a river, before the walk evens off into a more level approach to the lake along a bed of water-washed stones which appear to have been covered by the lake at some time in the past. These stones (some are almost perfectly round) are not exactly good news, the legs and feet being already tired from the exertions of the Tizi Ouanoums. Looking up at the valley sides there are stone shelters for goatherds and their animals. Thin trickles of smoke revealed that some were occupied.

The lake is reached after what feels like hours walking across the rock and boulder-strewn valley floor. Many circular patches have been cleared of stones to make camping easier on the northern shore, and Brahim's practice was to erect a tent in which to prepare a meal. The group would normally take the opportunity to have a swim. The lake's height at 7,529ft

(2,200m) is low enough to be quite hot during much of the day in the summer. The light coloured rocks also radiate a great deal of heat. Around the shores tidemarks of scale show the varying levels of the lake. This is due primarily to seasonal water flow from the mountains, but is also a result of the demands placed on the waters of Ifni for irrigation in the fertile valley below.

With the air of a magician Brahim produced a battered old fishing rod from somewhere, and I went with him to try our luck. He put a small shiny spinner on the line and we walked round to the eastern flank. I did not hold out much hope but Brahim knew the waters well. Within an hour we had a dozen or more freshwater trout. None were particularly big, mostly measuring 5–6in (14cm), but when fried they really were delicious. None of the Berbers like to linger on the shores of the lake for too long. Strangely enough, neither did the trekking groups. Although they seemed a perfect resting place for the night they were not welcoming. Brahim told me that according to local legends the shores are peopled by djinn, or spirits. I never felt completely relaxed there.

On one occasion, Lake Ifni very nearly caused a disaster. One member of a group had an inflatable airbed to sleep on at night. When we arrived at the lake he inflated it and threw it onto the water. Since it was a hot day the muleteers joined the group for a swim. Most were good swimmers but one of them had never learned. He held on to the airbed for support, kicking wildly with his legs. Meanwhile a wind blew up, and most of the swimmers came out of the water to eat. Some time later we heard a cry from the centre of the lake. It was the muleteer. Unseen he had been blown right into the middle of the lake. He seemed to be trying to kick his way back towards us but he was obviously weak. At that moment Ifni looked frighteningly big. It is also extremely deep. One of the muleteers began to cry, saying over and over in

High Atlas village perched above terraced fields.

delighted to put up our groups. The village always welcomed us warmly and it was a relief to rest from the rigours of the climb over from the Mizane. The villages of the south part of the High Atlas range are different in many ways from those in the north. The pace of life is slower, and the emphasis slightly more on the traditional mixture of terraced cultivation and animal husbandry. Villages such as Aroumd are inevitably influenced by easy access to Marrakesh and Asni, but for a village like Amsouzart the bright lights are a long way off.

The houses of Amsouzart are magnificent. Many of them stretch up to five stories and they are superbly crafted from the best stone and timber. (Wood supplies seem to be more readily available in the south, perhaps the northern

Village scene in the High Atlas.

French that the boy would die. Brahim went white as a sheet. If the airbed deflated, the boy would sink like a stone. The sun went in behind a bank of grey cloud at that exact moment and waves began to appear on the surface of the lake. Fortunately, in the group was a Scottish draughtsman who was impressively fit. He swam out into the middle of the lake and towed the muleteer back to the shore. The boy was in a state of shock and took days to recover. I noticed that he never accompanied any of my groups to Ifni again.

The best night-stop in the Ifni region is in the village of Amsouzart, at 5,708ft (1,740m) down the same valley which is fed by Lake Ifni. Brahim had an excellent contact there who was

Merchants on the way back from market at sunset.

slopes have suffered more rapid deforestation.) Another feature of Amsouzart are the walnut groves. The nuts can be seen in their various stages of treatment before ending up as part of our Christmas celebrations. They fetch high prices in the markets of southern Morocco, being a crucial part of the cash economy of the Atlas villages.

As the trek progressed I decided it would be too easy to run the groups as self-sufficient units. We could certainly cook for ourselves, as many groups do, and stay away from the villages, but we were in danger of ignoring the Berbers. By staying in the villages and buying local produce, we would, albeit in a small way, be a part of the community. We could also make sure that we helped the village as a whole by buying chickens from one man, tomatoes from another, the couscous from another, and so on. So many groups just rely on one food source in remote mountain villages, enabling one or two families to benefit whilst the rest receive nothing from the influx

of wealthy walkers. The groups were certainly keen on this idea but there were drawbacks which became rapidly clear. The first was that our diet would vary enormously in substance and quality. In some villages we would be able to buy meat and vegetables easily, in others we would eat nothing but rice and oil. And after a hard day's walking, the prospect of a plate of plain rice is not amusing – for that is precisely how the Berbers live for much of the year. The second disadvantage was that local food meant, for some, stomach upsets and illness. It was rarely very serious but 24 hours of the 'Marrakesh quickstep' can seem like an awfully long time when there is no toilet in sight!

In contrast, our evenings were fun and interesting. The women in the group would often learn about the daily lives of the Berber women. It always seemed harder to find out what the men actually did beyond sitting in the shade of the walnut trees talking! The ritual serving of food was always elegantly done. First, a jug of water would be circulated for the washing of hands. Then the steaming feast would arrive. The head of the household would remove the lid with a flourish to reveal couscous, rice or tagine. Tagine (a Berber stew) is cooked in a special clay pot, and is a frequent dish in the High Atlas, being marvellously filling after a day on the trail. Freshly baked bread is also often available in the villages.

Sometimes we were fortunate enough to be present when they played music. By the light of butane gas lamps, we would sit in a circle and join in as the muleteers got into their stride. The music of the High Atlas is heavily reliant on a pulsating, frenetic drum beat which feels distinctly African. The lead voice chants out the verses, and the rest join in the chorus with the gusto of a football crowd. It was so stirring that come midnight our groups would still be singing and clapping even though the next day's walk was just six hours away.

From Amsouzart we headed north to the village of Tissaldai. This walk was always voted the most pleasant of the circuit, being on an even gradient along a charming valley with a gushing stream below. It has the feeling of a hidden valley, particularly as it culminates in a dead end at Tissaldai with some of the highest walls of the Atlas rising sheer behind. The only problem with this section of the trek was the dogs which guarded several of the small settlements along the route. One particular hamlet had a team of dogs that seemed intent on ripping us to shreds. They would block the path baring hideous slavering fangs, daring us to come one step closer. The bravest dog made darting forays at our legs and ankles. Brahim just laughed at our dismay and, picking up a fist-sized rock, threw it with great accuracy at the biggest animal. This scattered the pack and we passed by unscathed. Europeans have a curious reluctance to hurt an animal even when it is clearly out to hurt them. The Berbers have no conscience at all on this score.

Tissaldai, which lies at a height of 6,870ft (2,100m) is reached after an easy half-day walk. The river which provides its terraced fields with water is the Assif Tizgui. When the flow is strong a waterfall spills over the cliffs providing a welcome shower, that is if you like freezing cold water. The village is noticeably poorer than Amsouzart, but the people none the less welcome hikers. Our base in Tissaldai was an open-faced house with a stunning view down the Tizgui valley. To relax here with a glass of sweet mint tea was always a highlight of the Toubkal circuit. The sounds of the village would filter up through the walnut trees, children playing and shouting by the river, goats and cattle crying in the surrounding hills. The afternoons would be spent exploring the village and going on impromptu walks, normally up the flanks of Amrourough which lies south-west of Tissaldai, separating the Tizgui valley from the Ifni valley.

The next stage entails a long and dusty trail up towards the eastern flanks of Toubkal. The Assif Tizgui is followed for the first stretch and then a path branching to the north for the climb to the Tizi-n-Ounrar Imaghka. Tichki lies north-west of this point at a height of 12,312ft (3,750m) – confusingly, Brahim referred to the whole region as Tifni. On the ascent, not far from a collection of seasonal shelters or 'azibs', there is a tiny spring. There is just enough of a constant dribble to keep a group supplied during a lunch break which consists of our normal meal of sardines, tomatoes, onions and bread. The east flank of Toubkal presents a tempting challenge from this location but, having already tackled it from the west, I never found a group interested in another try!

The next overnight on this relaxed circuit was the remote collection of azibs marked on the map as Azib Tifni. Reaching them involved a descent of 1,968ft (600m) from the Tizi-n-Ounrar Imaghka. Throughout the summer these shelters are home to a fascinating, shifting population of herders. The grazing for their

Campsite at Azib Tifni.

animals is good, with large areas of flat ground and abundant water even in July and August. Each of the animal herds is guarded by a family unit that can extend to granny and all the children, everyone treating it as a summer holiday. It is a relaxing, beautiful location which epitomizes the timeless quality of the High Atlas. The area is perfect for camping, although sleeping out under the stars is a better option. Staying in the huts is another possibility, but you may end up sharing a sleeping bag with an assortment of High Atlas biting bugs.

From Azib Tifni there are two options. The first is to return via the Tizi-n-Tagharat to Sidi Charamouch. This col stands at a height of 11,292ft (3,440m) and involves a relatively

gentle walk up from Azib Tifni compared to the climbs to most of the cols in the region. The route from the top of the Tizi-n-Tagharat to Sidi Charamouch can be managed in anything from 1½–3 hours depending on your nerve for scree-running. From Sidi Charamouch it is a simple matter to walk back down the Mizane to Imlil or Aroumd. The longer, and in many ways more interesting route, involves crossing the Tizi-n-Likemt at 11,614ft (3,540m). This is achieved with a hard 3–4 hour climb from the collection of shelters at the bottom of the gorge (they are marked on the maps as Azib Likemt). The track runs up the left flank of the valley to the col, the traveller's reward being a drop into the Imenane valley where the village of Tacheddirt is reached.

There is an excellent CAF hut in Tacheddirt which most groups are delighted to use after variable and often cramped accommodation in the villages. A jeep track has been extended year by year up the valley so, by the time you read this, it may well have reached Tacheddirt. If so, much of the originality of this charming Berber village may have been lost. From Tacheddirt the final day of the circuit follows the Imenane valley down to the Tizi-n-Tamatert at 7,476ft (2,280m) where the descent to Imlil takes an easy couple of hours. Those wishing to extend the circuit can cross to Oukaimeden where there are opportunities for ascents to interesting giants of the High Atlas including Oukaimeden at 10,738ft (3,270m) and Angour at 11,863ft (3,600m).

And at this point the Toubkal circuit comes to an end, without doubt one of the finest routes in the High Atlas. The mountains offer the most exciting scenery, while the villages really are wonderful. As an introduction to the High Atlas, it cannot be bettered, and fortunately it is well within the capabilities of anyone who has an average degree of fitness.

Tassili Trekking
by Chris Bradley

For almost an hour the only sound was the tight rasp of heavy walking boots scuffing sandstone. None of us had the energy, nor inclination, for unnecessary conversation. There was no easing of the heat, the gradient, nor the pace set by our Touareg guide. Only occasionally would he stop to ensure tail-enders did not get lost in this maze of gigantic twisted stone towers, and allow us to quench our thirst with that most precious Saharan commodity, water.

The size of England, the Tassili n'Ajjer stretches from the Algerian oasis town of Djanet to the Fezzan in Libya, and rises 2,500ft (762m) above the rolling dunes and rocky expanses of the Sahara. Its name means the 'plateau of chasms', and since no vehicle can penetrate its difficult landscape the good news for walkers is that all visits must be made on foot. There is no easy access to the oldest rock paintings of prehistoric man.

The problems for lone walkers are considerable and start the moment you arrive at Djanet airport. The Air Algérie flight from Algiers is usually crammed with large groups of French and Italians. Outside it gets worse. Even though it is 8 a.m. in October the temperature is above 100°F (37°C) and there's a heat haze above the sticky tarmac. Tempers fray as an incoming group clashes with an outgoing one. They are quite easy to distinguish because the French in the Sahara wear more ski accessories! For my part, I have a group of seven seasoned travellers on this, my third visit to the area.

We brought most of our supplies with us since food availability and choice are rather limited in Djanet. Also, imported goods are expensive in Algeria, more so when the price is multiplied fourfold due to the low official exchange rate. Hamou the agent strolled up, issued a few directives to subordinates and we set off in the mad cavalcade of three- and four-wheel drive vehicles hurtling across the desert towards Djanet. Without a local agent this 15-mile (24km) journey could be really time-consuming, or an expensive taxi ride. Either way you must contact one of the several agencies in town before applying for permission to walk in the Tassili region. This is one of the ways in which the Algerians can monitor the whereabouts of foreigners, and help protect the widely spread sites of historical interest.

There is evidence that trans-Saharan trade was started by the North African Berbers as far back as 3000 BC using human porters to carry the goods. As the climate became progressively drier so agriculture and trade within the Sahara slumped around 2000 BC. Despite these drastic climatic changes trade continued because salt was required in the south, and gold and ivory in the north. The rock paintings of the region give but a brief glimpse of life during this period.

From AD 300 camels were used to transport larger cargoes with greater ease, some camel trains numbering several thousand animals with attendants, guards and merchants. Grain, glass and weapons were carried from the Mediterranean

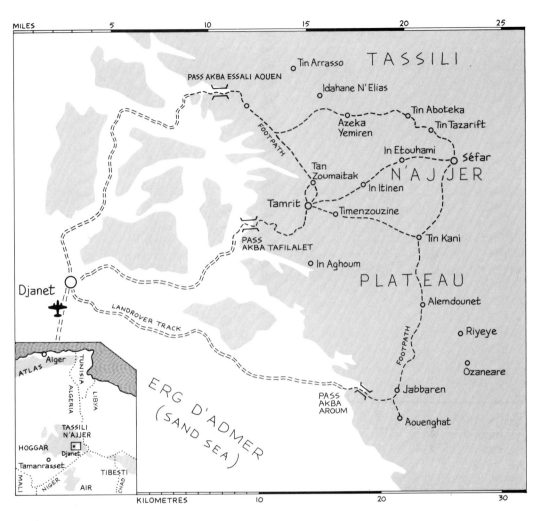

into the Saharan settlements and exchanged for local products such as dates, hides and, most important of all, rock salt. Continuing south these items found ready markets in the Sudan, an area that used to embrace the whole of west and central Africa. The rewarding return trip involved gold, ivory, slaves, ebony, kola nuts and ostrich feathers. Being at the crossroads of these major caravan trade routes the oases have always represented a microcosm of the continent with Chaamba, Touareg, Tibu and Berber intermingling at these green outcrops in the khaki desert wastes. Djanet (which has been described as the 'most beautiful oasis in the world') is surrounded by the massive Tassili plateau, the Erg Admer sand sea, and the Ténéré desert, and has three distinct settlements. The Senussi came from eastern Libya via Fezzan, the Tibu from the mountainous Tibesti region, and the Touareg nomads of the Tassili and Ahaggar ranges.

As rainfall is rare the water for the oasis is hauled from deep wells using donkeys, ropes and pulleys. Small, well-kept well-watered gardens

55

Two Touareg in full ceremonial dress celebrate a festival in Djanet.

(in Arabic, 'djanet' means garden) produce wheat, barley, vegetables and dates so that the oasis is virtually self-contained. But this does not mean it can supply all the requirements of the tourist trade, especially when large groups, are concerned. The distinction between traveller and intruder is very fine, and relies much on the attitudes and experiences of the local people. In general it is better for groups to supply their own needs, rather than stretch the resources of such remote places. However, the small 'souk' just off the main road can provide a limited choice of fruit and vegetables.

The town was a pleasant enough place to complete all the necessary paperwork, having a laid-back atmosphere, but it does not warrant an overnight stay unless this was part of a trans-Saharan trip. Permission to visit the Tassili region must be gained by a personal visit to the OPNT (L'Office du Parc National du Tassili), accompanied by a representative of one of the local agencies who will act as guarantor during your stay. The officials also require passport details, the daily itinerary, precise bivouac sites, the name of your guide, and your job description. Do not make the mistake of bragging that you are a photographer or journalist, otherwise you run the risk of not being allowed to continue on the grounds of your commerical activities! If you are journeying by yourself it would be best to visit all the agencies in town to see if you can join another expedition. In all, contacting officials and agencies can be a lengthy procedure, particularly if you do not speak French or Italian. The only saving grace is that you can fill-in time visiting the nearby makeshift museum.

Having agreed to observe the regulations of the area, it was mid-afternoon by the time we were dropped at the foot of the Tafilalet Pass. The vehicles coped as best they could with the conditions but here nature is firmly in control, with any human activity being scoffed at by the sheer scale of monumental upheaval. Boulders, dunes and outcrops twist around each other, making even the shortest of journeys resemble a sweaty theme park ride in a sandstorm. From a distance the Tassili plateau looks like a solid wall of rock rising from the desert floor, but closer inspection shows it to be a warren of huge gorges continually cutting into the softer rock.

Next came a late lunch and a chance for me to organize the amount of food and water we needed to take on to the plateau for four days. By the end of the afternoon the steep-sided valleys had already cast deep shadows across our camp beside a wadi. A few dry, stunted trees were the only signs of life. The drivers returned to town, promising to bring more water the next morning. After the evening meal, we sat around talking, getting to know each other and exchanging travellers' tales. A Canadian, an American, a Malaysian, one Dutch and three British, all with very different reasons for visiting this part of the Sahara. As it grew colder we climbed into our sleeping bags, wrapped up in our thoughts and expectations. For some it was their first night in the desert. My main concern was the five-hour 2,200ft (670m) climb on to the plateau, and what Irene (our 60-year-old Canadian) had just told me. She had a plastic hip!

The sound of a bleeping alarm clock might be incongruous in the middle of the Sahara, but it is the only way I know of making sure that this tour leader gets up on time. At 5 a.m. in the pitch black and cold I prepared gallons of tea and coffee, ensuring breakfast would sustain us to the top of the climb. Half an hour later a few donkeys led by two Touaregs wandered in and by 6 a.m. everything was packed under the one good eye of our guide Mokhtar, a local of few teeth and even fewer words. He arrived as promised together with the jerry cans of water. One point that continually amazes me is the high quality of planning and reliability that exists here. In a place where time might have little

meaning, guides, donkeys, camels and vehicles always turn up as arranged (although usually from the opposite direction expected). Having worked too much in Egypt I enjoyed these certainties.

By the time we left the desert floor, early morning rays of sun were catching the rocky pinnacles high above the still dark valleys. The donkeys with the two minders carried the cooking equipment, water, and some of our baggage, and made their way up a long circuitous route of even gradient. We carried day sacks and water bottles, following Mokhtar up a series of climbs on a more direct assault. After one hour going steadily uphill it felt good to head deeper into the plateau along a broad wadi that slowly closed in to form a gorge with 1,000ft (304m) walls. From here we clambered across the bare rock, picking our way as best we could up the giant steps scored by the irregular rain action. On the trickier sections Mokhtar took great delight in showing Irene the best foot and handholds, her only concern being that she was holding the rest of us up. I, for one, was only too glad to have the opportunity of taking in such dramatic scenery at an easy pace. We tried to explain Irene's predicament to Mokhtar. Bemused, he nodded, and then tried to work out why the end piece of a plastic water bottle should be in someone's leg!

Theories abound as to why these uplifted areas look as they do. It might be that the present landscape is a relict, the causal action having occurred when the climate was very different: extremes of temperature; weathering by wind and sand; and erosion by rain and ice on the brittle sandstone have left a landform of deep canyons, craggy peaks and rock corridors. Tens of thousands of paintings in ochre schist are the only legacy of early attempts to inhabit this rugged region. Figures of elephant, antelope, giraffe, ostrich and leopard were painted until about 3,500 years ago, when the climate dramatically changed.

57

Trekking on the Tassili Plateau, Southern Algeria. (Photograph by Chris Bradley.)

The route to Tamrit, Tassili Plateau. (Photograph by Chris Bradley.)

After five hours we popped our heads over the lip of the plateau. It was noon, and the flat, baked sandstone surface shimmered in every direction. Sunglasses, sunhats and suncream were working overtime to stop us from frying. Another hour of steady walking, this time across uneven broken slabs, brought us to the tented camp at Tamrit. During the tourist season from October to April this camp is permanently manned and is the base for scientific groups in the area. The donkeys had beaten us to the bivvy site ½ mile further on, and were taking a well-deserved drink from the dubious looking 'guelta' (at the end of the summer most of the rock pools are either totally dry or very glutinous). After the morning's activities and lunch we were all quite happy to find a shady spot and wait for the heat to subside.

The whole area resembles a giant building site, with huge blocks, some angular others rounded, meaninglessly scattered across the landscape dwarfing our human forms. So deep and intricate are the gullies that even an ordnance survey map would be useless for making sense of the area, and we gratefully followed Mokhtar in the late afternoon as he led us to Tan Zoumaitak to show us our first examples of rock paintings. On the back wall of a large cave were brown and cream male figures wearing head-dresses and ornaments, surrounded by horned creatures. Everyone was suitably impressed, more so with the fact that we know virtually nothing about the people who painted them. On the way back we skirted around the top of a gorge that somehow must have linked up to the Tafilalet. Peering over the 1,500ft (417m) drop, I was glad we came the way we did.

In the evenings Mokhtar and the two 'donkey men' shuffled through the site wrapping their grubby 'gelabias' warmly around themselves, and sitting down by a small fire. In a place where there is one tree every thousand square miles if you are lucky, the Touareg are masters of firemanship. A bunch of twigs scarcely larger than matches will somehow produce enough heat to bake fresh bread in the sand, cook a meal for three, and boil sufficient water to provide sweet tea for 11 people over 5 hours!

Fiercely independent for centuries, the Touareg 'Kels' wandered these vast expanses of the Sahara Desert. They refer to themselves as the 'Kel Tagelmoust' – the People of the Veil, with the men and not the women covering their faces. The 'litham' is traditionally several pieces of Sudanese cloth sewn together, which when wrapped around the head leaves only a thin slit for the eyes, a practical choice of clothing when faced with the extremes of sun and sand in the world's greatest desert. Import restrictions rather than personal choice have forced most of these 'blue men' to abandon the indigo clothing, whose dye impregnated their skin.

The Touareg are still divided into different castes, some carrying their ritual symbols of dignity, a lance, sword and shield. Top of the list are the tall, light-skinned nobles of Berber extraction, the 'Imohar', to whom all physical work is anathema, and who would never deign to till the land. Second are their vassals the 'Imrad', who load the camels and make rope. Then come the serfs, 'Iklan' (non-Berbers), who tend the gardens and act as camp followers. There are also craftsmen known as 'Inaden' who make bowls or saddles, and who live separately from the rest of the group.

Today the Touareg are settling in and around the oases, using their knowledge of the desert to aid outsiders rather than terrorize them. They are also adopting a more pastoral lifestyle, political and economic changes forcing them (like other nomadic peoples throughout the world) to give up their wandering existence.

The next morning we broke camp at 7 a.m. and headed across the plateau towards the 'city' of Sefar where the greatest concentration of paintings exists. *En route* we inspected those at In Itinen and In Etouhami, which also provided useful resting places. We travelled across a mainly flat, rocky surface with gentle undulations, on which our feet would have been cut to shreds had we tried to wear Mokhtar's prehistoric sandals. Nearing Sefar the landscape changed yet again. The only way I could describe the scene is by likening it to a whole

Touareg of the Tassili region.

series of London Underground tunnels roughly at right angles to each other, bored into the crumbling rock just below the surface, with the roof having fallen in.

Amongst this surreal patchwork are 'streets' of curved walls full of weird human figures with disc-shaped heads, and even weirder fantastic animals. Some figures are simple outlines with little detail, while others are shaded in reds and browns or are stippled. Discovered by the French Lieutenant Brenans in 1933, during his country's occupation of the area, the rock paintings of the Tassili n'Ajjer have been systematically explored and mapped by Henri Lhote since 1956. In his book *The Search for the Tassili Frescoes* he sets out the four main artistic periods.

The first primitive paintings date from around 6000 BC characterized by giant humanoid shapes with featureless faces, and scenes of magic and worship. The Great God of Sefar that we were now gazing at looks down from the cave wall like a ghost frozen in the sterile atmosphere of the world's greatest open-air museum. The second period lasted until around 1500 BC

Rock painting at Sefar, Tassili Plateau. (Photograph by Chris Bradley.)

indicates a peaceful existence of herdsmen with domesticated cattle, and scenes of hunting wild animals (the figures were first carved into the rocks and then painted). A period of chariots and horses shatters these pastoral scenes as paintings show the Hyksos (Sea People) invading from Egypt. Their trail of destruction can be followed in rock paintings from Libya to Morocco. The final period is marked by the appearance of an animal that has remained above all the symbol of the Sahara, the camel, which was introduced from Asia around AD 300.

For unknown reasons the sites of these paintings were of great importance. Interestingly at Sefar and Jabbaren the paintings, separated by 5,000 years, overlap one another, whilst nearby large expanses of rock wall remain untouched. Since their discovery the anthropological, zoological and artistic content of the paintings has fascinated scholars. From 1978 the Algerian Ministry for Information and Culture, and

UNESCO, worked together to control this massive National Park and are still experimenting with varnishes to protect these priceless treasures from human and environmental pressures.

Returning to Tamrit by a different route the following day we bivouacked at the top of the Tamrit Gorge, which gave us the opportunity to see the rock carving of the elephant at Timenzouzine. It is unique because it is carved into a floor slab rather than on a wall. Having again waited for the main heat of of the day to subside we followed the line of ancient cypress trees on the upper part of the gorge. These 1,000-year-old trees are the only living link with the past and are found nowhere else on earth. Amusingly the locals maintain that they can recite their prayers twice before a stone thrown into the Tamrit Gorge hits the bottom, or until an irate Italian yells back at them!

In the winter months the night temperature

Gorge near Tamrit on the Tassili Plateau.
(Photograph by Chris Bradley.)

might well drop below freezing when a thick sleeping bag would be needed, but at other times a lighter one is better. After a filling breakfast we packed up and set off on the descent. We went at a steady pace since Irene was beginning to feel the effects of a few days' hard walking, and my knees always complain about going downhill too fast. Five hours later we reached the desert floor, grabbed a quick lunch, and set out in a four-wheel drive Toyota for a three-day excursion to the Ténéré and Erg Admer. Later we returned to climb the escarpment and visit the Jabbaren paintings. The site of Jabbaren – the Land of Giants – is 12 miles (19km) south of Sefar, and can be reached via Alemdounet along the top of the plateau, although this means carrying up even more supplies. By far the most popular route is a single day trek up

and down, spending about four hours viewing the paintings.

This is a straight three-hour climb up a boulder-strewn cleft with spectacular views across the Erg Admer sand sea. Since food and water for the day have to be carried by each individual, Irene decided to sit this one out! For the rest of us Mokhtar upped the pace to ensure sufficient time at the sites around Jabbaren. And what paintings – the famous hunter, legions of warriors, and herds of tended cattle. In the dry atmosphere the colours have deteriorated little, and only the vandalism by recent visitors detracts from some of the world's oldest artistic treasures. The paintings are to be found in groups, not far from the edge of the plateau. Here the terrain is still as chaotic as at Sefar but on a smaller scale. Looking south there are tempting views as the plateau breaks up and plunges into the desert before being lost in the hazy distance of Niger. The climb and the heat make this a tiring day, but worth the effort.

If a visit to Djanet is part of your trans-Saharan journey, then you will probably have enough time to wait to join a group, or until there are enough people in the campsite to make a group of your own and arrange a visit through one of the agencies. For those on tighter schedules, flying to Djanet is the only solution, and even then it would be well worth contacting specialist tour operators. Usually, first-time visitors to Tassili make the paintings the object of their trip. For second and subsequent visits it is, however, worth exploring more of this wild and beautiful area.

At the end of the journey I sat at the top of the Tamrit Gorge at sunset, and looked along the peaks of the Tassili towards Libya. The sun had lost its strength and the land was every colour from the brightest gold to the deepest black. Across the border was the Tadrart Plateau and beyond that the Erg Tin Merzouga. 'Anybody fancy joining me?' I asked. Irene thought about it, and eventually said 'Sure, why not?'

Hiking the Hoggar

If you like the idea of guaranteed sunshine and do not mind the occasional scorpion in your sleeping bag then the Hoggar mountains of the central Sahara are the place to be. Stretching for almost 500 miles (800km) on a broad east–west plane, the Hoggar effectively form the geographical centre of the Sahara. Not surprisingly, this is one of the least hospitable places on earth, but for the backpacker looking for something really different, it has a great deal to offer.

Reaching Tamanrasset, the nearest town to the Hoggar mountains, is the first task. If you are pushed for time it is possible to fly to Tamanrasset from Algiers, but by far the best way is to travel overland and experience the magic of the Sahara on the way. My companion for the trip was Barney Lynch, a long-time friend and fellow mountain enthusiast. For six days we travelled through Europe and across the Mediterranean to Algiers. From there we took local buses to In Salah, the 'gateway' to the Sahara, and then negotiated our passage on an open-top lorry for the 408-mile (660km) journey to Tamanrasset. A French traveller told us in a moment of conspiratorial confidence, 'Go for the oldest, most beaten up truck you can find, they always have the best drivers!' Whether his logic was crazy or he was having a laugh at our expense will never be known, but we certainly took him at his word.

In an obscure back alley of In Salah our eyes lit up as we found the vehicle of our dreams. The tyres were completely bald, the windscreen shattered in several places, the fan belt was made of knotted rags, and a steady drip of glutinous oil splashed on to the sand beneath from the engine. It looked as if it had served as a troop carrier in the Crimea, been bombed and abandoned by Rommel and then, after several trips carrying boulders from London to Sydney and back, had been snapped up by an enterprising Algerian to carry on the good work in the Sahara. Mohammed the truck driver was not exactly in pristine condition either and we viewed his scarred, grizzled features with trepidation, noting particularly his missing left eye and wondering what effect this might have on his driving abilities. Although Mohammed had been swift to accept our cash offer for transportation he was less rapid when it came to leaving. In the end we spent three days hanging around In Salah before his truck had enough goods to leave.

For five days Mohammed the veteran Saharan driver drove his truck towards Tamanrasset, and for five long days it consistently broke down at every possible opportunity. By the third day Barney and I had learned how to replace a propshaft, remove a broken leaf on a spring, and patch worn out inner tubes. By the fifth day we knew every component of the engine and injection systems intimately and were fully fledged Grade 1 diesel mechanics. We perched precariously on the top as Mohammed crashed the old Berliet down holes, piloted into rocks which would have stopped a tank dead in its tracks,

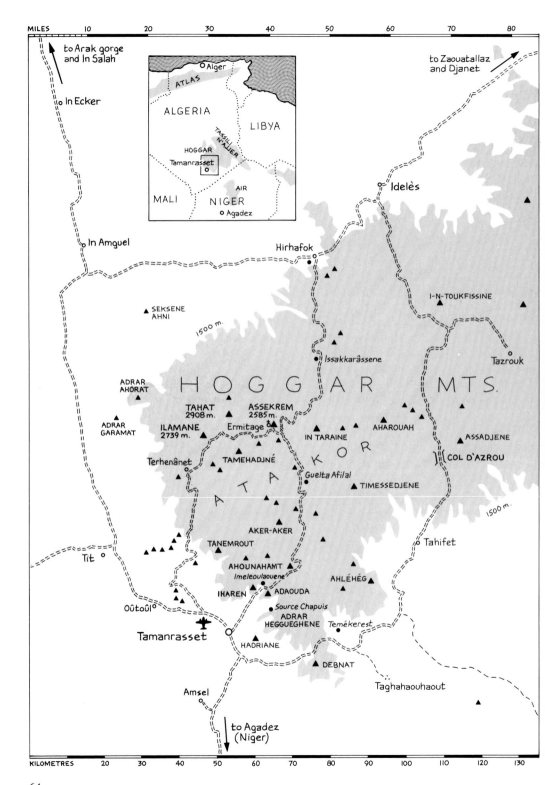

MILES   10   20   30   40   50   60   70   80

to Arak gorge
and In Salah

to Zaouatallaz
and Djanet

In Ecker

ALGER
ATLAS
ALGERIA   LIBYA
TASSILI N'AJJER
HOGGAR
Tamanrasset
AIR
MALI   NIGER
Agadez

In Amguel

Hirhafok

Idelès

I-N-TOUKFISSINE

SEKSENE
AHNI

1500 m.

Issakkarâssene

Tazrouk

ADRAR
AHORAT

H O G G A R   M T S.

ADRAR
GARAMAT

TAHAT
2908 m.

ASSEKREM
2585 m.

AHAROUAH

ASSADJENE

ILAMANE
2739 m.   Ermitage

IN TARAINE

K O R

COL D'AZROU

Terhenânet   TAMEHADJNÉ

A T A

Guelta Afilal   TIMESSEDJENE

1500 m.

AKER-AKER

Tahifet

TANEMROUT

Tit

AHOUNAHAMT
Imeleoulaouene

AHLÉHÉG

IHAREN   ADAOUDA

Oûtoûl

Source Chapuis
ADRAR
HEGGUEGHENE   Temékerest

Tamanrasset

HADRIANE

DEBNAT

Taghahaouhaout

Amsel

to Agadez
(Niger)

KILOMETRES   20   30   40   50   60   70   80   90   100   110   120   130

64

Transport to Tamanrasset — broken down again as usual.

this story of a 2,000-mile (3,220km) expedition from Chinguetti in Mauritania that had sparked my interest in the Sahara, resulting in the journey that Barney and I were about to undertake.

By Saharan standards Tamanrasset is a new town which has wasted no time in becoming the principle staging post of the area. Founded by the French as Fort Laperrine after their successful conquest of the Touareg tribes at the battle of Tit in 1902, Tamanrasset has thrived while the more ancient trading oases, such as Sabha, Bilma, Tombouctou and Oualata, have declined. The principle reason for the rise and rise of Tamanrasset is its geographical position right in the middle of the main north–south trans-Saharan route. Travellers arrive in great numbers every winter season expecting it to be every bit as romantic as the name implies.

Most visitors, though, find Tamanrasset a big disappointment. Where there should be bustling souks there are modern boulevards. Functional government buildings jostle for space and half-finished building developments occupy every spare plot. Bags of cement and steel reinforcing rods seem to fill every lorry that comes into town. Travellers in Landrovers and Toyotas pack the campsite and hotels complaining that there is no water, and truck loads of officious military personnel parade the town, scowling with ferocious glares at anyone foolish enough to look their way. Tamanrasset began life as a military fort and the Algerians seem keen to keep it that way. Even the campsite is subject to frequent 'raids' by military and police alike. Quite what they are looking for is never really clear.

Tamanrasset does have its charming side though, if you look for it long enough. It can be found in the smiling faces of the many Ghanians, Malians and Togolaise who form a shifting workforce in the town on their way to the Libyan oilfields. It exists in the shops where, in a quiet moment, one might meet a Touareg

and ploughed in low gear through deep sand. Very rarely did the truck exceed 25 miles (40km) per hour, and when it did, the whistling wind and unaccustomed 'G' forces made it feel as if we were going ten times faster.

The road marked on our maps was nowhere in evidence and it occurred to us that perhaps our route was one which avoided the endless checkpoints where Mohammed's papers could have been scrutinized by eagle-eyed officials. Our arrival in Tamanrasset supported this theory with Mohammed going to intricate lengths to creep into the town without being spotted. Eventually he stopped the truck and hissed at us. 'Descendez vous . . . ici c'est Tamanrasset'. The words could not have moved us more if he had announced Atlantis, El Dorado or the garden of Eden. It was a sheer luxury just to have stopped.

Over the next couple of days as we recovered from the truck journey we found that Tamanrasset is a curiously mixed-up place. It was here that Geoffrey Moorhouse ended his ill-fated trans-Saharan camel journey so movingly described in his book *The Fearful Void*. It was

Père Charles de Foucauld, holy man of the Sahara.

straight from the desert buying tea, cloth and sugar. And it exists in the great gatherings of camels in the wadi at certain times of the year. Our arrival coincided with one of these occasions when there were hundreds of camels waiting to be hired, sold or loaded for long journeys into the desert. Their guardians sat in huddles over burning embers, swapping news from perhaps as far afield as Zinder or Tomboctou. Walking through the haze of dust amidst the smells and coughs of the camels was a moment of intense, almost biblical, charm.

Over the following days the serious business of preparing for our trek began. Back at the campsite Barney spread out the only map of the area we had been able to acquire. It was the *Carte Internationale du Monde NF-31* from the IGN in Paris, and stated on top 'Tamanrasset, 1:1,000,000.' The scale was far too big for our purposes but we had to make do. In the middle of the map, clearly marked with the symbol

of a church or chapel, was the Érmitage du Père de Foucauld at a height of 12,480ft (3,800m). Our plan involved getting a lift to the Hermitage, with water supplies and food, and then walking back to Tamanrasset, exploring some of the most exciting parts of the Hoggar as we went. The distance recorded on the map for the 'piste' to the Hermitage was 45 miles (70km), but as we intended to return by a circuitous route and navigate by compass we reckoned we would probably cover nearer 62 miles (100km), allowing for getting lost. We had never heard of anyone else attempting the walk. Most of the travellers to whom we mentioned our idea thought us completely mad.

Every trek has its unique set of problems and normally one looms larger than the rest. In our case it was plain and simple – water. There were peripheral problems too, like the large scale of the map and the fact we would be walking in very high daytime temperatures, but the supply of water was the only one that seriously threatened our plans. Marked on our map were two tiny blue dots which represented two of the very few permanent water sources in the western Hoggar range. The nearest to the Hermitage was called Afilal. The other, closer to the Tamanrasset end of our route, was the unpronounceable Imeleoulaouene. In addition were several feint blue crosses which read 'Water point. Not identifiable on aerial photography.' We decided we could not rely on finding them.

How much water would we need? Barney reckoned 10½pts (6L) each per day, I thought nearer 14pts (8L). The Wexas *Travellers' Handbook* offered the following advice on the subject: 'Dehydration is best expressed as a percentage loss in body weight, 1–5 per cent causing thirst and vague discomfort, 6–10 per cent causing headache and inability to walk, and 10–20 per cent delirium leading to coma and death'. Since we had no way of measuring a percentage loss in body weight, this alarming intelligence was pretty useless. The handbook went on, 'assume that an average unacclimatized man working out of doors in extreme hot/wet or hot/dry conditions will drink 7–9 litres (12–16 pts) of fluids per day.'

Taking the most pessimistic view that our consumption would be 16pts (9L) per day, that would mean an incredible 79pts (45L) each for our planned five-day walk. We realized there and then that whichever route we took would be based on a journey which would link the two permanent water supplies, even though that would mean crossing the 'piste' and perhaps meeting vehicles. When we revealed this plan to a French traveller who had seen the two water sources or 'gueltas' we were relying on, he told us that both were very low and surrounded by animal droppings. They were little more than stinking, slimy green pools. It was not welcome news but at least we had a camping stove to boil the water, if we could wait that long for a drink!

To try and solve the question of water, we decided to have a test day walking from Tamanrasset past the volcanic plug of Iharene. We walked fully laden for about four hours in the morning, and then four hours again in the afternoon under a crystal clear sky. We regretted not having a thermometer with us. Not a cloud passed overhead. It was our first experience of walking in the central Sahara and by the end of the evening, having returned to the campsite, we were quite tired. The effect of walking through soft sand had been hard on calves and feet alike. We kept a careful tally of our water consumption both for drinking and cooking (washing was out of the question). By the end of the day we had consumed 19½pts (11L) between us.

We worked out new calculations based on this figure and realized we still needed more water-carrying capacity. As a result we purchased a couple of extra 3½pt (2L) plastic bottles. Whilst in town an Australian told us that the only way to keep our water cool was to buy a goatskin water container or 'guerba'. He assured us that the water inside was kept refrigerated by latent heat loss as liquid evaporated through pores in the skin. As chance would have it he could even sell us one, having completed his trans-Saharan journey from Agadez. A deal was struck and we became the proud owners of a rather scabby looking goatskin which we christened Gordon. Draped across our shoulders, Gordon could contain an additional 17pts (10L) of water for the trek. At least, that was the idea. A trial sip from the infernal thing revealed that it did, as the Australian entrepeneur had warned us after purchasing it, 'Taste like a dingo's armpit'.

A friendly Italian family in a Toyota Landcruiser gave us a lift up to the Hermitage. It was our first real view of the Hoggar. What a place! It is commonly described as lunar but I have always thought of the moon as a rather stark and boring landscape. The Hoggar comes straight from the canvases of the world's great surrealists.

67

Drinking from the 'guerba' goatskin container. Every last drop was carefully conserved.

They are so Daliesque in the way peaks unexpectedly jut out of a perfectly flat plateau that a science-fiction writer would feel at home amongst them. They look as if they have been baked for a few million years too long in a cosmic oven. In the wadis were stunted trees and shrubs, but otherwise no vegetation. A shimmering heat haze swallowed up the Toyota as we commenced the breathtaking switchback ride up towards the Hermitage at Assekrem. Behind us a plume of yellow dust lay suspended in the air like the vapour trail of a jet.

Next morning we climbed to the stony col of Assekrem before dawn. This is the place that Père Charles Eugène de Foucauld chose for his Hermitage, which has stood here since 1911. He wrote: 'The view is more beautiful than can

be expressed or imagined. The very sight of it makes you think of God, and I can scarcely take my eyes from a sight whose beauty and impression of infinitude are so reminiscent of the Creator of all; and at the same time its loneliness and wildness remind me that 'I am alone with Him.'

Born in 1858 at Strasbourg, de Foucauld spent the first years of his military career earning the unenviable reputation of being little more than a slob. Tales of his gastronomic excesses are legendary and he was often overweight. His string of mistresses were clearly not deterred by his nickname – 'the pig'. When his regiment left for Africa in 1880 he took with him his lover Mimi, creating such a scandal that he was dismissed from active service the following year

One of the spectacular volcanic plugs of the Hoggar.

'for lack of discipline and notorious miscon-duct'. He then began to study Arabic and Berber dialects and made long horseback journeys into the Kabylie mountains of nor-thern Algeria. It was a period in which de Foucauld life's found a new direction. As Anne Fremantle wrote in *Desert Calling*, her 1950 biography of him: 'Charles had acquired, bet-ween December 1880 and March 1881, an in-delible love of Africa, ot mountains, and of the Berber people.'

Disguised as a Jew, the ex-dilettante made a long and perilous journey through Morocco and soon became a man of God. His time as a Trap-pist novice gave him the chance to think about his destiny and, at the age of 42, he became a priest devoted to the work that he continued through the rest of his life, bringing Christianity to the vast territory of the Sahara so recently conquered by the French. He vowed to shun all worldly goods and eat as would a beggar in the street. Although he seemed a hermit, de Foucauld spent much of his time with the Touareg tribes of the Hoggar. He realized that to

convert them to God, he must first understand their lives, their traditions and their language. In an age when the common European view was that Africans were little more than savages, this was an extraordinarily enlightened approach.

Just one of the remarkable achievements of Charles de Foucauld was his compilation of a four-volume French-Tamashek dictionary. Writ-ten in his own neat hand, and printed complete with his crossings out and corrections he made, it is still the most complete work on the langu-age of the Touareg. He also wrote down in English many of the love poems and accounts of epic battles they traditionally recited to each other. As with everything that de Foucauld did, this was an act of complete devotion. I was very moved when Christine Goyheneche, a great Saharan traveller, recently sent me a copy of the four-volume dictionary out of the blue. If I owned a library of a million books, none would give me more pleasure than Père Charles de Foucauld's *Dictionnaire Touareg – Francais*.

Ironically, Père de Foucauld was killed by the very Touareg he sought to convert. The end

The Hoggar Mountains seen from the Hermitage of Père de Foucauld.

came in 1916, close to the Hermitage in Tamanrasset which had now become a fort. He was shot by a 15-year-old boy, but his name lived on in his native France. To this day he is regarded by the French as a national hero, his memory being cherished rather in the same way that the British cherish the memory of Lawrence of Arabia. Films and books have tried to capture what made de Foucauld such a charismatic figure, but his real monument lies on the col at Assekrem, a small stone chapel, testimony to the faith of a man devoted to the Sahara, its peoples and the God he found there.

The Hermitage nestles in the midst of some of the greatest peaks in the Hoggar. To the east is I-n-Taraine at 8,845ft (2,690m), to the west lies Hamane at 8,986ft (2,740m) and a little to the north lies Mount Tahat, the highest of the Hoggar at 9,540ft (2.9km). Also nearby is the volcanic plug known as Ilamen, a vertical rocket of a peak about which the Kel Ahaggar,

the Touareg of the region, have many superstitious beliefs. We saw all these sites as the dawn broke over the Hoggar. It was cold, and one of the Little Brothers of Jesus who still occupy the Hermitage gave us blankets to keep warm. The mountains looked wonderful, each moment of changing light painting new colours on to peaks, ridges and jagged silhouettes. Barney, a catholic, celebrated mass in the chapel and we left the Hermitage eager to start the walk.

Shouldering the packs, we left the Assekrem col feeling as if we were stepping off the edge of the world. In our packs were the basics for survival. A cooker and pot, lightweight utensils, a Swiss army knife, small medical kit with plenty of suntan cream, matches, ultra-lightweight sleeping bags, tea and coffee, sugar, salt, a few dehydrated meals and dates. In addition there was a flysheet with poles and pegs, and we also had the luxury of two books for the long hours

The hot walk back to Tamanrasset. (Photograph by Barney Lynch.)

we knew we would be spending under the flysheet during the heat of the day. And finally there was the water supply, either inside the packs or sloshing around inside Gordon the goatskin. We had one final glimpse of the tourist vehicles in the car park beneath the Hermitage, and then we were on our own.

The first and most noticeable effect was the adrenaline kick that comes with any adventure, but which is particularly sweet if you are tackling a new project. Of course the Hoggar are regularly tramped from north to south and from east to west by the Touareg in search of new pastures for their herds, or as they journey from one camp to another. But that did not alter the potential for adventure that we were looking for. We could take any route we chose, camp in isolated wadis, search for rock engravings, even go scrambling up the more accessible peaks. It is the freedom of movement in a wilderness that gives this type of self-sufficient walking such an

exciting edge, and was in marked contrast to the tourists confined in their air-conditioned vehicles on their way back to Tamanrasset.

Our main problem was the phenomenal heat. This was August in the middle of the Sahara desert, with the Tropic of Cancer just to the north. We had read in Jeremy Swift's superb book on the Sahara — in the series *The World's Wild Places* — that temperatures in the summer can soar to 122°F (50°C) in the shade and that sand temperatures of up to 175°F (79°C) have been recorded. He concluded, 'There is probably nowhere else outside of the polar regions so hostile to most forms of life.' Feeling the moisture in our mouths dry out almost immediately, we made sure we drank regular small amounts of liquid. Despite our 'familiarization day' back at Tamanrasset, we knew the most critical period of acclimatization would be the first couple of days so we covered our heads with turbans and liberally plastered on suntan cream.

71

With the turban wrapped close to the face, in the style favoured by the Touareg, the breath is bounced back at the lips keeping a moist pocket of air in front of the mouth. What many people assume to be a culturally determined piece of clothing is actually very practical, although the Touareg are well aware of the striking image of a man who reveals nothing but his eyes. But if the men are veiled against the heat, glare and dust, then why not the women? We never found the answer.

During the halt in the middle of the day we lay under the flysheet, and looking around us in every direction could not see another scrap of shade. As the sun moved overhead we were forced to shift position to keep the shade on our legs and arms. A heat haze shimmered above the rocky surface which looked thick enough to walk on. Curiously, in motion, we had found that we did not seem to sweat at all. This was an illusion created by the immediate evaporation of our body fluids. Under the flysheet, though, it was different, and the sweat ran freely across the body. We ate dates and cooked pint after pint of sweet black tea but we could never avoid the heat. It did not just come through the plastic flysheet, it radiated from nearby rocks and reflected off the sand. No matter which way we turned, a wall of scorching air was waiting to envelop us. Not the slightest hint of a breeze came to our aid. It was too hot to do anything but eat and think about bathing in a swimming pool filled with ice.

By 3 p.m. we were restless to be off, even though it seemed just as hot as at midday. We climbed onto a small nearby peak and took compass bearings on the greater identifiable peaks around us. One of the Brothers at the Hermitage had shown us a much more detailed map of the area, so we now had a hastily scribbled copy to refer to. The route we took was along a prominent wadi (unnamed on our map), one of the many which drain from the highlands of the Hoggar. For months on end, perhaps years,

these wadis lie dormant, almost as if they have forgotten how to flow. Then, after a sudden downpour, they spring to life again, bearing water with all the urgency of an Alpine meltwater stream. Some of the wadis from the Hoggar drain for enormous distances into the Azaouagh valley in Niger. This is the biggest wadi in the Sahara desert and it runs straight into the River Niger not far downstream from Niamey. It was an exciting thought that we could be walking in the headwaters of one of the world's longest watercourses.

We had heard that water could be found by digging at low points in the wadi, but try as we did we found nothing but dry sand. A few stunted shrubs were dotted about the sandy floor, all showing evidence of having been heavily cropped by animals. A couple of spindly trees looked as if they might give some shade, but when we approached there was a carpet of thorns beneath them which acted as efficiently as barbed wire in keeping us away. The only life to be seen was the scarab beetle and the ubiquitous 'desert robin', a small black and white bird which has the same opportunistic tendencies as its European cousin when it comes to scrounging food from humans.

Towards sunset we headed on a more easterly bearing which took us towards the water source at Afilal. The temperature dropped rapidly after 5 p.m. and became almost pleasant. Only the swooshing sound of the water in the bottles on our backs and the pat of our feet on the rocky surface broke the silence. When we stopped it was so quiet we could hear the blood pumping around in our bodies. Mountain trekking is normally a noisy experience, there always seems to be wind moving through trees or rocks, or a stream running in a valley far below. In the Hoggar there is no sound at all, it is almost as if the mountains are holding their breath.

As night fell, we cooked rice, and pasta, and sardines. It was a meal at which the average alley cat might have turned up his nose, but for

The flat plateau land of the Hoggar. Crossing this was the hottest day of our lives.

us it was five-star cuisine. A handful of black pepper thrown in by Barney added the final touch. And then, for the first time that day, a thin layer of cloud made an appearance just before sunset. Shortly after, it was completely dark, with just the stars shining in a moonless sky. We had worried that the evenings may be boring with no torch to read by (in our fanatical attempts to save weight we had ruled out a torch as a luxury), but the stars proved an entertainment in themselves. Lying beneath them, tired out by the day's exertions, we looked for shooting stars. They came with surprising frequency every few minutes.

By noon the next day we reached the permanent water source at Afilal. People had warned us to beware of the Algerian military who were active in the area, so we approached with caution. With our water supply now down to 3½pts (2L) we desperately needed more if the walk was

to continue. A large sign translated as 'Tourists Keep Out' had been erected on the track, and a high ridge of sand and stones blocked the entrance. It looked bleak. We could see a couple of uniformed soldiers lounging in a tent not far off but since they did not see us, we continued walking down to the pool. It was a beautiful spot. The water was clear and fresh and a thick mass of vegetation surrounded it. We hurriedly filled our containers and turned to leave. It would have been nice to stay and explore but we did not want a brush with the military. Once they found out we were on foot they may have tried to stop us. Crossing the track once more we headed west towards Takoukait. Far away in the distance was the squat figure of Aker Aker, a uniquely uniform rectangular peak with a flat table top. Finding a faint track across the plateau, we carried on to the south-west.

The session under the flysheet that day was

73

particularly unpleasant, with the sun redoubling its efforts to fry us alive. We read as slowly as possible to conserve the books, and Barney spent most of the afternoon boiling the Afilal water so it would be safe to drink. We were drinking enormous quantities now, more than our water ration would allow. As I drifted off to sleep, the only sound registering in my mind was the steady drip, drip, drip of water splashing onto the desert floor.

DRIP! At the same moment we both leaped to find the source of the leak. It was Gordon, the traitor, leaking away our precious water. How much had we lost? We had no way of measuring but it was certainly several pints. Gordon had been nearly full after our stop at Afilal and now he was half empty. With at least two days' walk to the next water source we had a serious water problem. From then on we resolved to drink the water from Gordon first, leaving the supplies from the more reliable plastic containers for later.

By 3.30 p.m. we were off again through trackless terrain. Picking a way through the rocks was tedious and a twisted ankle was always a possibility. Then, suddenly, Barney spotted three white dots in the distance. A look through the telephoto lens on my camera confirmed that they were gazelle. They had seen us almost immediately and ran off as we crept forward for a closer look. How the dorcas gazelles can survive in the Sahara is nothing short of miraculous. Not only do they have to find vegetation to feed on, but they are hunted by the Touareg. In fact, in many parts of the Sahara they have been virtually wiped out. We had been told that these gazelles have become so highly adapted to life in the arid Sahara that they rarely, if ever, need a drink. All their liquid needs are supplied by vegetation. It was a sobering experience to realize how hopelessly and badly we were suited to the desert, with our massive reservoirs of water strapped on our backs. Of other life there was little sign beyond a discarded viper skin, a

scarab and the occasional spider or ant. They were the only clues that life can survive out here. We had worried about scorpions but, even though Barney spent hours turning over rocks and poking around in likely holes, we never saw one.

We had now descended a long way from Assekrem and the wadis were cutting deeper into the land. Often when we arrived at one we would leave the packs in a shady spot and walk up the sandy bed for a while. After the sterile, rock-strewn landscape even the most humble shrub or scrappy tree seemed outrageously lush and green. It was on one of these exploratory wadi walks that we came across camel tracks. Following them we came into a wider area where there were a few trees and low-lying vegetation. A dozen or so camels were grazing in the valley and two Touareg were lying nearby under a tree. They had seen us long before we saw them, and greeted us warmly as we approached. They seemed not the least bit surprised to see two backpackers miles from the tourist 'piste'. Neither spoke any French but we managed to understand through sign language that they had come up in search of their missing camels. Both had the look of the true nomad, so different from the 'town' Touareg of Tamanrasset who is more streetwise. A small leather bellows was then produced from a saddle bag and used to rekindle a tiny fire that was smouldering nearby. Long, gracile fingers broke mint and sugar into a battered blue pot which went onto the fire with a satisfying sizzling noise.

Much has been written about tea ceremonies in the Sahara. They are lengthy, filled with unwritten protocol and rules, but the underlying principle is one of great hospitality. Our friends assumed, as a matter of course, that we had the time to spend a couple of hours with them. All our anxieties about water, blisters and heat evaporated in the company of these men who eke a precarious living from the Hoggar. They

Touareg camel herders near Tamanrasset.

were from the Kel Ahaggar tribe, one of the many Touareg confederations in the Sahara. Now their livelihood comes from animal husbandry and whatever they can grow in the gardens of the oases, but in the past a raid or 'rezzou' was an important feature of life. The caravans that passed through the Hoggar were rich with ivory, gold dust and slaves. A 'tax' might be imposed by the confederation chief or 'amenokal', or the caravan taken by force. Touareg poetry is filled with accounts of famous raids, and you cannot help feeling that they do lament the passing of those wild days.

It was so relaxing in the shade of that tree that we decided to abandon any hopes of more progress that day. Our deadline was only self-imposed so why not break it? The hours slipped past easily in the company of the two Touareg as

we communicated in sign language drawing maps in the sand. They showed great interest in our equipment, examining the camping cooker with delight. Their own belongings were simple and practical: a blanket, teapot with glasses, tea, sugar, dates, dried joints of meat wrapped in a greasy cloth, and a quantity of couscous grain. We slept around the dying embers of the fire, our two Touareg friends talking energetically into the early hours.

Next morning we parted company. The Touareg mounted their camels with great style and continued ever deeper into the Hoggar in search of their lost camels. We shouldered our backpacks and struck south for Aker Aker. In our water containers we had just 5pts (3L) of warm water, while Gordon had 3½pts (2L) of rancid sludge swilling around his guts. There was no choice now but to head for the next water source in one day. We estimated it would take us eight hours hard walking with no prospect of a midday stop. It was bad luck that this particular session of the walk should coincide with the most treacherous terrain. The plateau we had to cross was peppered with a carpet of irregularly shaped boulders and rocks. There were two techniques, to try and pick a way through them, or to skip across the top of them. Barney chose the first, I chose the latter. Both ran the risks of a bad sprain or twisted ankle, and both found it impossible to gain a regular walking rhythm. The ominous pain of impending blisters nagged away in our overheated feet.

During the hottest hours of the day we walked around the monolithic mass of Aker Aker. Originally we had hoped to climb on it but there was no prospect of that now. Speed was of the essence. Every half an hour we stopped and drank a strict ration of one cup – it was not nearly enough to conquer our thirst. By mid-afternoon we had exhausted all the supplies in the plastic water containers. The moment had come to drink the dregs. It was a measure of our ferocious thirst that we could even consider drinking the foul-tasting muck that Barney now poured out. Goat hairs and dead insects polluted it, but at that moment we could not have cared less. We drank it all.

A few miles to the east was the main 'piste' from Tamanrasset. It would have been easy to walk over, wait for a vehicle to pass and ask for water, but we had promised ourselves that we would finish unaided. It was interesting, having spent most of the day in a state of thirst, to feel our bodies go into a new stage of what might be termed 'super-thirst'. Neither of us had known such a state before. Every particle in our bodies seemed to be crying for water. We were losing

body fluid through evaporation at a phenomenal rate. All our thoughts were directed towards the water source we knew we should reach that evening.

At last the plateau channelled into a narrow defile where we were briefly forced to take to the jeep track. No vehicles passed us and finally, about one hour before sunset, we walked into a deep-cut canyon. It was filled with more plants and animal tracks than we had seen in the whole trip. Following the canyon, we came to a dead end with a stepped series of water-eroded rocks. In a downpour one could almost imagine it being a waterfall. And then, those at the bottom of the wall, was the sight that we had pinned all our hopes on, a pool of deep, clear, water. We had arrived at the guelta of Imeleoulaouene. Kneeling at the water's edge we put our lips to the surface and drank like animals straight from the pool. The rest of that night was spent in a state of complete exhaustion as we boiled up water for tea. We drank gallons, recycling the tired old tea bags which were all we had left.

Our feet had taken a battering and the forced march had given us both blisters. We bandaged them up as best we could and set off the next morning for the final haul back to Tamanrasset. We were not looking forward to returning to the town. Our brief trek through the Hoggar had shown us a side of the Sahara that nobody will ever see through the windows of a four-wheel drive vehicle. We had experienced walking through one of the most arid mountain ranges on earth. There had been moments which we would never forget – the two Touareg on their search for camels, the gazelle that survived against all odds, and our arrival at the Imeleoulaouene guelta. We had touched, albeit briefly, the magic that drew Père Charles de Foucauld to this surreal and beautiful range.

Hot Days in the Anti Atlas
By Chris Bradley

Of the mountain ranges in Morocco, the Anti Atlas occupy the most southerly position. They lie to the south of the wadi Sous, and to the west of the wadi Draa, stretching down to the coast in a south-westerly line. The mountains to the east of the Draa are commonly known as the Jebel Sarhro. Although the highest point of the Anti Atlas is only 8,303ft (2,530m), the mountains are fascinating to explore, and have a totally different feel to the High Atlas.

My journey to the Anti Atlas began with a cheap charter flight to Casablanca and a train journey to Marrakesh which was fast, comfortable, and excellent value for the four-hour trip. That night there was plenty of time to soak up the atmosphere of the Djemma el Fna, still throbbing with drummers and dancers even though this was August and the heat was intense enough to melt the tarmac on the roads. From here it would have been easy to head into the relative cool of the High Atlas but the thought of summer hiking in the Anti Atlas was too tempting.

Early the next day I tried to beat the system by catching an express bus to Agadir rather than the SATAS service direct to Tafraoute. No matter how long you spend wandering around Africa and the Middle East, you always forget when you return on a subsequent visit that things happen differently out here. I had made the grave mistake of using logic. I should have known better, because in the end I found myself catching the same SATAS bus in Agadir, only by this time I could not find a seat. Through the hot summer afternoon this mobile sauna lurched and rattled forever southwards, sweat and dust caking itself in alternate layers on my body. The slightest breeze that disturbed the broiling muggy atmosphere was greeted with yells of disgust, backed up by tuts of approval. By late afternoon we had passed over the Col du Kerdous, the site of a new deluxe hotel with spectacular views, and by sunset had bounced into Tafraoute, the heart of the Anti Atlas. All the while I had been enquiring about bus times for the return trip, so that I could make the best possible use of my stay.

Of the two budget hotels, I first checked out the Tanger and immediately decided on the Redouane across the road (this decision was based purely on the melting point of bed frames!). The restaurant, balcony and reception area was one of those edge-of-the-desert crossroads that attracts the strangest groups of people. Lounging around were some very laid-back Europeans soaking up the atmosphere, whose idea of a walk meant finding the nearest bar. Down in the restaurant I met an English couple.

'Trekking!' she exclaimed, 'I'll tell you about trekking.' Apparently it was their first time out of Europe, and they had come to the Anti Atlas because of a friend of a friend's recommendation. 'It was horrific' she added. In five days they had managed 3½miles (6km) of trekking, which had put them off for life. 'I almost died'

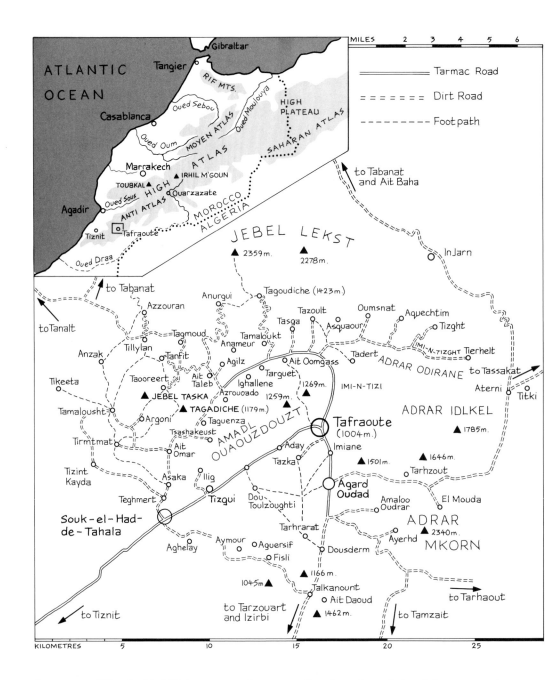

MILES   2   3   4   5   6

════════ Tarmac Road

= = = = = = Dirt Road

- - - - - - - Footpath

ATLANTIC
OCEAN

Gibraltar

Tangier

RIF MTS.

Oued Sebou

Casablanca

HIGH
PLATEAU

Oued Oum

MOYEN ATLAS

Oued Moulouya

Marrakech

ATLAS

SAHARAN ATLAS

IRHIL M'GOUN

TOUBKAL

HIGH

Ouarzazate

Agadir

ANTI ATLAS

Oued Sous

ATLAS

MOROCCO

ALGERIA

Tiznit

Tafraoute

JEBEL LEKST

Oued Draa

to Tabanat
and Ait Baha

▲ 2359m.   ▲ 2278m.

InJarn

to Tabanat

Anurgui   Tagoudiche (1423m.)

to Tanalt

Azzouran

Tasga

Tazoult

Oumsnat

Aquechtim

Tizght

Tagmoud

Tamaloukt

Anameur

Asquaour

IMI-N-TIZGHT   Tierhelt

Anzak

Tillylan

Tanfit

Agilz

Ait Oomgass

Tadert

ADRAR ODIRANE   to Tassakat

Tikeeta

Taooreert

Ait
Taleb

Ighallene

Targuet

1269m.

IMI-N-TIZI

Aterni

Titki

Tamalousht

JEBEL TASKA

Azrouoado

1259m.

ADRAR IDLKEL

Argoni

TAGADICHE (1179m.)

Taguenza

AMADL OUAOUZDOUZT

▲ 1785m.

Tirmtmat

Tsashakeust

Aday

Tafraoute
(1004m.)

Imiane

▲ 1646m.

Ait
Omar

Tazka

▲ 1501m.

Tarhzout

Tizint
Kayda

Asaka

Ilig

Agard
Oudad

Amaloo
Oudrar

El Mouda

Teghmert

Tizgui

Dou
Toulzoughti

ADRAR

Souk-el-Had-
de-Tahala

Tarhrarat

Ayerhd

▲ 2340m.

MKORN

Aghelay

Aymour

Aguersif

Dousderm

Fisli

to Tarhaout

1045m ▲

▲ 1166m.

to Tiznit

Talkanount

Ait Daoud

to Tarzouart
and Izirbi

▲ 1462m.

to Tamzait

KILOMETRES   5   10   15   20   25

she went on. They had left Tafraoute one day at noon to walk the 2 miles (3km) to Agard Oudad and back. In the heat, it took them three hours. 'Rather you than me' she ended. I thanked them for their invaluable advice and ordered food elsewhere.

On the edge of the Sahara in midsummer there was little doubt that it was going to be hot, where even at night the temperature rarely sent you into a sleeping bag. I checked with the locals on the availability of water in the villages on my proposed route and calculated accordingly. Walking alone, I made sure that the hotel reception knew of my first destination. Tafraoute lies in a depression about 3,280ft (1,000m) above sea level, totally surrounded by rugged mountains. To the south is the main peak of Adrar Mkorn at 7,677ft (2,340m), beyond which the landscape flattens out to become the Sahara. To the north is a ridge of mountains called Jebel Lekst rising to 7,739ft (2,360m). The main road along which I had travelled ends at Tafraoute, from where several smaller roads wind their way up and through the jumbled lower slopes. Just to the north of the town, and arcing around it, is the 12-mile (20km) long Ameln valley – the area of my trekking would be bounded by the road in the valley, and the Jebel Lekst peaks.

I woke when it was light at 5.30 a.m. I had a quick omelette and coffee and I was walking through the waking desert town before sunrise. Once away from the bone-dry fields of the village I scrambled up and over low rocky outcrops of granite to reach the Ameln valley. A seasonal river (January to April) flows here, as does a road linking a string of small villages. I crossed this road at Ait Oomgass, and took the opportunity of buying fresh bread, cheese and tomatoes from the local shop. These would be my only provisions, apart from about 1 gallon (4.5L) of water; I had cut down on the carrying weight, relying on food available in the mountains and the generosity of the locals.

I was immediately struck by the scenic beauty of the area which included rose-red Petra, the Tassili plateau and the central mountains of Yemen. A series of small, steep wadis run into the Ameln, and it is usually at the head of them that small hamlets cling to the sides of the mountains. Beyond Ait Oomgass the track zigzagged its way up the dusty, red, iron-rich slopes beyond Tamaloukt. My plan was to climb to Tagoudiche before the main heat of the day, find somewhere to stay, and make a quick assault in the late afternoon to the top of Jebel Lekst, the highest peak of the Anti Atlas west of Irherm. Around, above and beyond Tamaloukt I walked, and by 9 a.m. my clothes were dripping with sweat. Whoever wrote that the heat here was dry had not visited in August! The dirt track clung to a ledge as it wound up a wide valley into the heart of the mountain. High above I could see a building perched on the very edge. The later the hour, the less shade there was, even in such a steep-sided valley, and I was glad to have my three 'suns' with me – sunhat, glasses and cream.

At 10.55 a.m. I passed the house on the edge, and got my first view of Tagoudiche, a collection of multi-coloured dwellings tumbling down the mountain side, one on top of the other. By 11 a.m. I was downing 1½pts (1L) of warm coke at the village shop. Mohammed was smartly dressed in white gellabiya, with the obligatory moustache and yellow slippers, and after a quick chat he took me to another Mohammed, the local schoolteacher. As the children were on summer holiday he allowed me to stay in the new schoolroom. Through the heat of the day villagers came in and out, and we chatted about everything – their lives, my life, my walking route, their families. My basic French was working overtime trying to cope with the conversation, and occasionally I would manage some Arabic that overlapped with their Berber language. As soon as they found out that I had been in Mexico to see the 1986 World Cup game between England and Morocco, and I had mentioned the names of a couple of Moroccan players, I was a friend for life.

Even at 3 p.m., my planned departure time for the peak, the temperature hovered around 114°F (45°C), so I waited for another hour. With my small daypack I headed out of Tagoudiche along a farmer's trail. Slowly but surely the overgrown terraces disappeared and I was working my way up a boulder-strewn hillside sometimes spotting what I thought could be a path. In the heat it took me two hard

Hiking in the Anti Atlas. (Photograph by Chris Bradley.)

hours of wild scrambling to reach the summit. Mohammed the teacher had said that Agadir could be seen from the top. The heat haze made this impossible, but I could make out the sandy orange tint of the desert in the opposite direction.

It took me almost as long to descend. Being alone I was aware that the slightest slip could be disastrous. Many tourists come here to walk in the winter, especially in February when the almond trees are in full blossom, but it might well be weeks before the next person came up here in summer. I took the greatest of care, protecting my suspect ankles and condemned knees as much as possible. The muezzin was calling the faithful as I staggered into the village at sunset. Arriving at the schoolroom I found it locked, with the teacher apparently at prayers. I did not mind waiting 10 minutes or so for him to return, so that I could get out of my sticky wet clothing, but in the end he did not return for another 1½ hours due to a special prayer meeting. Even after that I could not wash, as the water supply was so low. I had decided to go to sleep early and forget about my dishevelled appearance, so I was more than surprised when the teacher invited me to join him at a wedding festival being held at the other end of the village, a couple of hundred feet away.

With no electricity, a torch was essential to find our way in the darkness. Climbing steps and twisting around houses we eventually came upon a small clearing brightly lit by bottled gas lamps. On three sides were dwellings, the other being a bare rock face with steps cut into it, at the foot of which four men slaved over huge steaming cooking pots. The area was carpeted and matted, with male guests sitting around outside. More men kept arriving, some in gellabiyas others in western clothes, and shook the hands of those already there. Every 15 minutes or so a low wailing sound could be heard that progressively grew louder, until the cause of the noise — a group of women — arrived from

another part of the village and made their way up the stone steps into the bride's house. The 21-year-old bride was marrying a man from Tsashakeust, further up the valley. These were the festivities for her family, the groom having his celebration at his village simultaneously. The next day the bride's family would go to Tsashakeust where the wedding would take place.

When about 50 men had gathered there was much shouting and gesticulating as we took it in turns to have our hands washed. Low circular tables were brought out and the food began to arrive. First of all we ate from a large dish of couscous and a bowl of almond juice. Each man moistened his hand in the juice and then took a section of couscous, popping it into his mouth. Next came the 'tagine' on an even bigger plate, consisting of lumps of mutton piled high upon mounds of potatoes, onions, pulses, tomatoes and beans. With this we had round loaves of bread, freshly baked. This was followed by a tray of melon slices, and the elaborate tea pouring ceremonies that took almost an hour. Just before midnight we had the post-meal hand washing ceremony and were sprayed with scent.

A rather bloated audience was then led in prayers, which combined traditional recitals and impromptu preaching. For the next two hours the men chatted or dozed, while the women were served their food on the rooftop of the adjoining house. Sporadic drum banging and shrieks came from them as they began to enjoy themselves. Meanwhile the bright hissing gas lamps attracted moths of every size and type. They swooped and circled until, drifting just too far away from the light, bats picked them out of the black sky.

Eventually, around 2 a.m. the entire group of women, numbering about 70, joined the men. All were dressed in their finest black flowing costumes, trimmed with gold and silver sequins, with only a hint of their beauty seen in flashing eyes. Grouped together the women provided the sounds of drums, tablas and piercing yells, the younger ones teasing the boys with alternate displays of dancing and coyness. The women swirled to the hypnotic beat, their monstrous eerie shadows cast against the ochre-coloured walls. By 3 a.m. I could not keep my eyes open any longer, and wandered back to the schoolroom. As I drifted off to sleep I could still hear the booming drum and the shrill voices echoing around the dark village.

After three hours sleep I was up again at daybreak, ready for what would be my most demanding day. Most hikers visiting Tagoudiche would now head back the same way and proceed along the Ameln valley before striking up another valley. I am always reluctant to retrace my steps, and had asked the villagers about getting across the side of the mountain to an unnamed village on my map (in fact, Anurgui). I had also kept a look out during my Jebel Lekst excursion for a path heading that way. Possible but difficult, came the replies.

Some 15 minutes out of Tagoudiche, I left the route ascending Jebel Lekst and followed a disused path up a series of steps into the next valley. There was still the remains of some terracing, but beyond that the path was almost totally lost. I headed for a crack in the valley wall to climb into the next one, most of the route being steep gradients on loose rocks. At the col between the two there was a stone marker, followed by several others. The walking here was most pleasant along a series of paths surrounded by various cacti and stunted prickly bushes. Although it was still early morning, I was beginning to sweat profusely.

I expected to see Anurgui in the next valley, but all I found was a deserted shell of a house and a vague track heading over yet another col. After two hours I caught my first glimpse of the village, a collection of no more than 20 buildings huddled into a narrow cleft in the steep valley. I replenished my stocks of water in Anurgui and headed down the valley towards

Agilz. I had been told it would take me 40 minutes. After half an hour I reached a high viewpoint that indicated this timing to be drastically wrong. It was almost 11 a.m. and the heat was intense. I thought of finding a shady spot under a rock for a few hours, but I would still have to descend to Agilz, and I might then run out of water. Onwards and downwards I trudged cursing the heat.

By noon I had just about reached the floor of the Ameln, and my dripping body just didn't want to be pushed any further. In the distance a few palm trees offered the promise of some shade and water. Decidedly weary, I staggered around the trees until I found a small well, with some very rough-looking, oil-stained water at the bottom. The track I wanted for the late afternoon led from here, but there was no way that I could get anywhere without more water. I poured the well water over my head, and sloshed to the nearest house, fortunately only 15 minutes away.

The women of the house looked me up and down in amazement. How could humanity sink so low? I must have looked a desperate case. Not only did they give me water but they brought me tea, then a plate of couscous with vegetables, and a mug of milk. It did the trick. By 4 p.m. I had had a sleep, filled my water bags and thanked them profusely and was ready to head off into the mountains again, this time towards Tanalt.

From the top of Jebel Lekst the previous day I had seen this track quite clearly snaking its way up the dusty barren valley. After an hour I came upon a crossroads of tracks. Two women and a man were collecting water from a large sunken water tank. One of the women offered me almonds and some prickly fruit, that, when peeled, is quite refreshing, despite being 90 per cent pips. Through Tagmoud the light was fading, and in Tillylan it was almost dark. The only light I could see came from higher up the mountain. Thinking this was in fact Tillylan I climbed further and discovered a group of men

Collecting water from well near Tagmoud. (Photograph by Chris Bradley.)

who had apparently been watching me for some time. They seemed amazed by my account of the day's walking, and all offered me accommodation for the night in their village of Azzouran. In the end I stayed with a man called Aazza who was on a month's leave of absence from his job as a hotel porter in Paris.

One fact that had struck me wandering through this region was that the inhabitants were relatively wealthy. In an area of isolated villages with sparse cultivation and extremes of temperature, the people were well-dressed, well-fed and certainly well-housed. Aazza explained this was because the men were traditionally shop owners in the larger towns of Fez, Casablanca and Tangiers. After years of hard work they would return to their villages, convert fortunes into land and houses, sire a new generation of shop owners, and take early retirement. Nowadays the men tended to work abroad instead, mostly in France and Belgium, as manual labourers. The traditional Berber-style house for Aazza and his family was large and well-equipped. It was the only one to have electricity supplied by French solar panels on the roof. He made sure that the rest of the

villagers knew he had a TV set by playing it full volume on the balcony. Sitting in front of it we had a simple but filling evening meal. The 'tagine' was accompanied by a dish of 'audi', a tasteless, thick ghee, and 'amnouz', a tasty, sticky-brown almond paste.

At night, with no moon, there was just a dark void beyond the balcony. But by early morning light the tiers of mountains rippled their way south in misty stages in a breathtaking panorama. Somewhere below, past Tanfite, was the Ameln valley, to the right Jebel Taska, and further around, a white tomb of a religious marabout on a hilltop. Beyond Tillylan and Azzouran an intriguing series of paths and dirt tracks meander around the mountains to Souq Talata, Tanalt, and beyond. However, my route was southwards down a narrow gorge following the Ait Soab, and helpful Aazza made sure that I started down the right descent. For an hour I picked my way down a dry river bed, ending up more often than not on a dry terrace, high above the chaotic rocks. Occasionally I passed small farmhouses, tucked into the folds of the valley, the dogs sensing my approach long before I could spot them.

Mules are still the mainstay of agriculture in the mountains.

After three hours I arrived at the village of Anzak, and gratefully drank a cup of cold water offered by a family. It was only when I was draining the dregs at the bottom that I noticed the cup was alive with wriggling larvae. My morning walking stint finished with a sprint session to Tamalousht. This Tamalousht — not to be confused with Tamaloukt near Ait Oomgass — is beautifully situated by a bend in the wadi. There were palm trees, neat groves of almond and olive, and rows of houses terraced up the hillside, many recently constructed and newly painted. In all there were about 200 inhabitants, said Mohammed at the local shop. We sat and chatted as the temperature soared. At noon he closed up and offered me shade in his house. To my surprise a large 'tagine' appeared just before my departure at 4 p.m. The hospitality of these people is superb.

From here the wadi made wide sweeps around the mountains, and I picked my way as best I could up and over the protruding spurs of rock. The seasonal river straightened out and I headed down the dry rocks of a wide valley. The huge boulders provided valuable shade for a few creatures. Dark pools of stagnant water bubbled as my approach caused a mass eruption of frogs half-buried in the mud alongside. This in turn prompted a display of small leaping fish, all trying to avoid the frogs.

Tirmtmat is another small village at a bend in the valley, just before the wadi enters the Ameln. There was no shop at which to meet the locals, so I was directed to one of the three large houses on the west bank. There was one-eyed Hamid, his son Abdullah, his beautiful inquisitive daughters, a dog called Lux, gallons of tea, a feast of a meal, and a flat roof to sleep on. What more could anyone want? Unfortunately the flies land on your mouth and nose about 10 minutes before sunrise. By the time I had packed, Abdullah arrived with breakfast, a bowl of 'azgeef', tea and biscuits. Made from the same semolina base as couscous, 'azgeef' is a type of warm runny porridge, exactly what is required before a day's walking. It was after 7 a.m. when I waved farewell and clambered up the hillside behind their house. From the top of the ridge I

The village of Tirmtmat. (Photograph by Chris Bradley.)

could see the Ameln swinging in from the left, with yet more punctuated foothills to the right. I managed to stay up high above the Ameln until a broad valley barred my route, and I had no choice but to drop down into the village of Asaka. I was offered a lift by a local, but turned it down by saying that I was on holiday. A string of small hamlets led me to Souq-el-Had-de-Tahala, where the dirt track through the Ameln joins the main road from Tiznit to Tafraoute.

From 10.15 a.m. I waited four hours for the Tiznit bus to tear past fully laden. In the end, I stayed another night in Tafraoute which gave me the opportunity of walking to Agard Oudad to see 'Le chapeau de Napoléon', rocks not really shaped like hats, and the weird paintings called Rochers Rocks. My penultimate night in Marrakesh, and a train to Casa for the return flight, brought a remarkable seven days to an end.

If you are the kind of person who does not mind turning up at a place unannounced, unsure of where you will sleep, then the Anti Atlas is for you. You might find you are offered a night on a roof or a private room in a luxury Berber house. In this respect I would strongly recommend the area above the Himalayas. It is also equally interesting and remote, but definitely easier and cheaper to reach. After a flight to Agadir there is just a four-hour trip to Tafraoute. Bear in mind too that the summer is hot but bearable, the winter cool and busy. Whatever the time of year, though, the locals will extend a warm welcome for those willing to take the time and effort to climb into the mountains. I am only just beginning to discover the excellent hiking opportunities in Morocco, but better late than never. Next time I will quickly go up to Tillylan and see if there really is a route through Tanalt to Ait Baha.

Walking with the Dogon

A Wake in West Africa
by Stephen Pern

The stars were still in the sky as I threw off my single sheet of homespun cotton. A penned donkey brayed, the harsh echo rebounding from the looming mass of the escarpment behind me. It was cool, too early yet for the dawn procession of women picking their way down to the wells, but this was May, the Moon of the Red Sun, and by midday the rocks would be too hot to touch. As subsistence farmers, the Dogon of Mali live precariously.

A compulsive wanderer through west Africa, I had heard of the cliff-dwelling Dogon, and their remote homeland, on the southern margins of the Sahara, long before I paid them my first visit. But this was to be a trip with a difference: instead of my usual, long, foot safari I was to settle down in the Dogon village of Tireli, my base for a four-month study of these desert-edge farmers and their arid environment. I was especially interested in their burial rituals, an interest which led me many hundreds of miles through the roadless wastes of Dogon territory.

A grumbling belly of cloud had hung low over Bamako, Mali's mudwalled capital when I left in a rented truck. To the south the annual rains had broken, but heading north across 500 miles (800km) of gasping savannah I stole an eight-week march on the wet season. Cresting a dune early on the third day my French-speaking driver had suddenly stopped. Implacable in the distant haze was a single landmark, the cliffs of the Bandiagara escarpment, rising in places a sheer 1,000ft (304m), a 120-mile (193km) long fortress wall. It divided a vast rocky plateau from the sandy plains that stretch interminably southeast to Mali's border with Burkina Faso. Strung along a 90-mile (144km) stretch of the cliffs are the most traditional of the 300 odd villages of the Dogon. In theory Tireli was somewhere nearby.

With a labyrinth of fallen rock at their backs the Dogon occupy a superb retreat in time of war, a natural defence which accounts for the sustained integrity of their culture. I knew of the Dogon custom of walling up the dead, and as we bounced towards the escarpment I studied the passing cliff face and the scree, hoping for a glimpse of dark burial tunnels. I saw absolutely nothing until the driver suddenly veered left and in French, the lingua franca of Mali, said 'Voilà, c'est Tireli'.

The camouflage of cliff-shadow and stone had been almost perfect, but now, abracadabra, the homes of 2,600 people leapt forth in a trick of the light, hundreds of flat-roofed adobe huts flung like bricks across the upper slope of the scree. Nothing was square, nothing symmetrical on this haphazard terrain, the mud-walled compounds so juxtaposed that roof followed floor down the jumbled rock fall, a honeycomb of huts bonded tight to a chaotic surface.

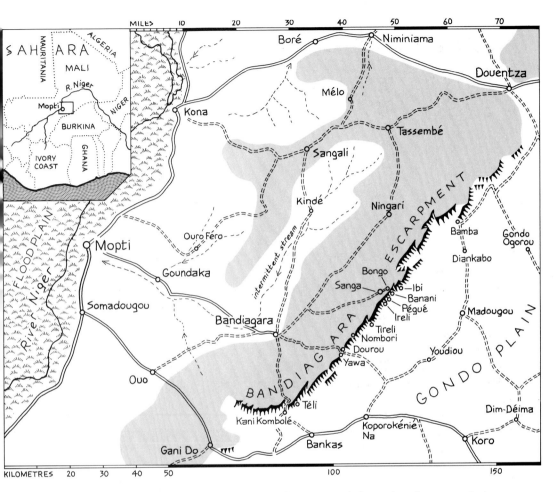

Now two months later, Tireli had become my home, my subconscious adaptation to the rhythms of village life complete. I knew every path up the fissured cliffs, and with the permission of the village elders had set about exploring long eroded routes to the higher caves. My first trip had almost been my last, sweat pouring from me in the 120°F (48°C) heat, sparkling in free-fall to the rocks in the village 300ft (90m) below. Using the rickety posts which long-dead generations of tribesmen had jammed into the cracks as booms for swaying up corpses, I eased on to the first of the narrow ledges I had marked for exploration. It was empty. Disappointed I had crawled to the next and peered in. Something

white erupted from the gloom, exploding towards me. As I reeled back, fighting for balance, the apparition became an owl and soared off into space, doing precisely what I was trying desperately to avoid.

Sick to my wobbling kneecaps, I hung on and crept into the tunnel. A sweet smell mingled with the stirred-up dust, and the small white objects that littered the tunnel floor snapped beneath my knees. Owl pellets, I thought, as I picked one up. Yet it looked more like a middle-size vertebra. Then came my second shock. I was crawling on a carpet of dry human bones. Time, I thought, for a breather.

From my eyrie high on the escarpment I saw

87

Bandiagara village below Sangha cliff.
(Photograph by Ann Peskett/Viewfinder.)

tiny dust devils twirling across the desiccated savannah that makes up over half the Dogon territory. The remainder stretched away, above and behind me over the rugged Bandiagara Plateau whose quartzitic sandstones tower so dramatically. Towards them rolled the ocean-like plains, wave after wave coming in from the haze to rise in freeze-frame just short of the cliffs in a crest of 100ft (30m) high dunes. Like a sea-cliff the escarpment fell sheer to a scree slope of colossal boulders, the rubble in places piled halfway up the face. It had been difficult to accept that the secret of human survival in this harsh land lay within the faulted massif itself. Though impervious, the conglomerates and sandstones are riddled with sinkholes and faults

that link into seepages along the base of the cliffs. It is this permanent water supply that enables the Dogon to remain year-round in their ancient village sites.

Two months into my study I had learned much and travelled far, but I had yet to see a burial itself. It was for this reason that I had risen so early. The previous evening I had heard the explosions of muzzle-loading rifles with which the Dogon announce a death. The corpse lay in a village 1 mile (1½km) along the escarpment. A faint breeze stirred the baobabs, trees as near to the shape of a beer bottle as it is possible to be, although to the Dogon baobabs are more than magnificent shapes. In this unforgiving land the powdered leaves are a staple food. Even the broken seed pods which litter the villages survive no longer than the arrival of the next goat.

It was not as food that the baobabs would be significant today. I did not yet know it but it was the bark, artfully stripped and twisted into ropes, which made the next hours so special. Slinging an empty goatskin on my shoulder I made my way down the boulder-strewn slope to the track under the dunes. Others were coming, wraith-like, over the rocks, the men in hand-woven tunics and caps, the women in indigo-dyed cotton. As dawn flared in the eastern sky we exchanged the customary greetings which, two months earlier had seemed so laboriously prolonged. Now the ritual exchange had become a familiar start to the day.

Other voices floated up from the gloom of a 15ft (4.5m) crater dug in the sand. As the dry season advanced these wells had been dug deeper and deeper, yielding the brackish, gritty water with which we now filled our goatskins. Beyond the next village, 1 mile (1.5km) down the track, there would be no more water for 9 miles (14.5km). Our waterbags filled, we waited no longer, padding away as the first rays of the sun drew deep orange from high on the cliff. An unheard of honour for a European, I was on my

Sangha cliff, Bandiagara escarpment. (Photograph by Ann Peskett/Viewfinder.)

way to a Dogon funeral. The growing light revealed quite a crowd on the narrow path. This, I felt was a way of walking almost lost to Europeans – the natural progression of human feet going about human business. You did not need boots or rucksacks or tents and you did not need to dress up. An everyday African journey is a low-key event, just the sound of a baby on its mother's back, and the shadow of a headload gliding through the bush accompanied by heat and dust.

My friend Dougulu turned to hand me the split half of a kola betel nut. I stored the astringent mush, hamster-like, in my cheek, and we followed a none-too-permanent footpath through the tree-studded sands. Soon the rains would come and the narrow routes would change. Established rights to cultivation, dormant in the dry season

would be invoked and where we now walked would be a sea of green millet. New paths would emerge as people picked their way round the sprouting plots, to be abandoned in turn after the next harvest, the more direct routes again possible.

When we reached Amani we found scores of people crowding the open square. Swathed in a chequered blanket, Yogojo's body had been lashed to a bier of spindly poles which was suddenly jerked into the air by a dancing mob of young men. A great wail went up from the women in the throng. As the men pushed each other aside to dance with the bier held high over their heads, an elder turned to the drummers.

'Beat out the "Rhythm of the Road"', he ordered above the din, 'We're going.' It was 7 miles (11km) to the dead woman's home

Market scene in Mali. The Malians are some of the friendliest people in Africa.

village of Nini. The old Amani men who would not be making the journey raised their sticks in salute. 'You came here to our village,' they shouted, 'and you gave us a son. You left a man with us, and we people of Amani now thank you.' Earlier that day a little of the dead woman's hair had been cut and stirred in a calabash with the contents of a sacrificial goat's stomach. One of the older men had been charged with dribbling the potion on both sides of the track to Nini. The Dogon believe that a dead body is potentially harmful to the new crops planted along its way. The libation would cancel out any harm emanating from the corpse.

The throng moved off behind the man with the calabash. Scuffles developed as young men vied to carry the body. To drop it would be an utter disgrace. A man from the village of Komakan had fallen while carrying a bier some 60 years ago, and the shame still afflicted his family. Despite the apparent chaos, the route

taken on such occasions was precisely defined by tradition, and the calabash man stopped many times to check that he was correct. Details such as boundaries and footpaths were ignored. Growing millet was trampled where it had been planted over the time-honoured route.

The carnival atmosphere was infectious. This was more like a charity marathon than a funeral procession, and I sensed, as I so often have in Africa, the subtle erosion of my individuality. Europeans are so bent on private achievements, on being the first or the fastest. We touch each other in very few ways. Africans, I thought, have a different and richer approach to life. And here they were, dancing for 9 miles (14.5km) with an old woman's corpse, being simultaneously joyful and sad.

As we passed the cliff villages on the way to Nini, women came to pay their respects. Approaching the village (built like Tireli on the scree below the cliff) the rhythm of the drums changed to one associated with women. The old lady had come home. She had left behind her role as a wife and a mother and was now as she had been born, a daughter of the village. Men came forward to greet us. They took the bier from the Amani boys most of whom then turned back. I slipped into the procession, climbing up behind the village towards a narrow valley running back into the plateau. A man tried to stop me at the mouth of the cleft but the leader of the procession intervened. He loudly declared that since I was a Tireli man and had come with the corpse all the way from Amani it was absurd to turn me back. I stayed.

A party went ahead to clear the barbed undergrowth that choked the path leading to the base of the sheer outcrop. We removed our shoes in respect for the place and followed. The bier was gently put down beside an alcove full of small pots. A fresh one, full of the oil of lannea seeds was placed there for the dead woman. A spindle and a small wad of raw cotton were placed beside it. 'When you go to the market' the leader intoned, 'take this oil for your feet and spin.' With the aid of a long bamboo pole, a baobab bark rope was looped over a beam jutting from a recess 30ft (10m) above our heads. Six young men climbed the rope to the ledge. Others removed the layers of blankets in which the body was wrapped, attaching the rope to the tasselled ends of the innermost. The wooden frame was cast on to a pile of several hundred others, the lower ones twisted and rotted with age. Yogojo's spirit would not be alone. The shrouded corpse nudged the cliff face as it was slowly hauled up and then eased through an opening in the mud-walled ledge. There among the bones of her ancestors Yogojo was laid to

Women pounding millet, Bandiagara region. (Photograph by Ann Peskett/Viewfinder.)

River scene in Mali.

rest, a small bowl of oil at her feet to ease them after the journey. The opening was carefully bricked up and the folded shroud tossed down. It hit the rocks with a dull thud.

On our way back to Tireli that afternoon the sky turned the colour of lead, the few sheep and goats scattered in the bush unnaturally white against the ripening sky. Thunder seemed to unfetter the wind, and the trees were obscured in the whirling dust. That night the sky burst. The rains had broken early. The first drops hit us 1 mile from home. The earth shook under the colossal weight of the storm. The temperature fell dramatically and for the first time in two months I was actually cold. Dashing forward I leapt the dusty gully beside Tireli market place. In just half an hour it had become a river 3ft deep.

For the time being the walking season in Dogon country was over. The time had come to repay my hosts with a few weeks of hard work and, instead of a notebook and pen, I carried a hoe. But the season for farming on the edge of the desert is short and the enigmatic escarpment the Dogon inhabit would wait. There would be time soon for other slow walks, village to village, time to watch life in the Dogon unfold.

Mount Cameroon

The year 1990 saw an explosion of interest in the west African country of Cameroon. The reason? The World Cup. No African team had ever progressed so far in the competition. By reaching the quarter finals, the Cameroonian team put their country on the map. Suddenly, English papers were dispatching reporters to this distant land. They sat in village bars and recorded the locals' reactions as the national side forged miraculously on. Not long after the World Cup, I left England for Cameroon. With me was Kees 't Hooft (his first name is pronounced 'Case'), the respected Dutch mountain cameraman and climber. We had often discussed

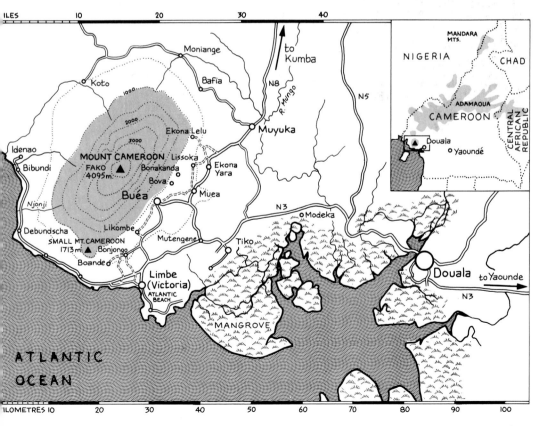

the idea of climbing Mount Cameroon and, at last, an opportunity had arisen.

At Gatwick airport the Cameroon Airlines 747 Kombi cut a dash of exotic promise. All around were the mean little charter jets of Dan Air, Iberia and Britannia packed with holiday-makers heading for the cattle market charter-lands of the Mediterranean. Out of this undignified rabble rose the elegant nose of the Cameroon jumbo, its bright red lettering con-veying an almost carnival atmosphere, aided by the green, yellow and red stripes on the side. Just looking at it gave us a buzz of excitement. The spotlessly clean plane seemed to be saying to all those Europackage planes 'Huh! Look at me, I'm going to Africa!'

However, it did so only after an incredibly long and tedious stopover in Paris. Kees was absorbed in Roland Huntford's biography of Sir Ernest Shackleton. This was a lingering hang-over of Kees's recent expedition to the remote island of South Georgia where he had been part of a team climbing unexplored peaks in the interior. It was odd that Kees's mind should still be on the glaciers and icebergs of the Antarctic as we headed for the tropical summer of the Bight of Benin.

I, with an eye for topicality, was immersed in Dervla Murphy's book *Cameroon with Egbert,* her account of a gruelling and incident-packed journey through the highlands. We dined roy-ally and drank a bottle of Bordeaux. Kees re-vealed epicurean tastes by ending with a glass of prune armagnac, a tiny glass of armagnac filled to the brim with, needless to say, a rather large prune.

When we arrived at Douala airport it turned out to be only half the nightmare we had anti-cipated. Health formalities, immigration and a chaotic customs check passed smoothly enough. It was humid, but not unbearably hot. And in the terminal were two splendid reminders that we were in Africa. The first was the crowd of touts, hustlers, 'helpers', and trainee taxi arrangers

which greeted us as we walked our first few steps from the terminal. The second was an extremely fat man in a pinstripe suit who was waiting patiently as a shoeshine boy energetically polished his dark tan leather briefcase.

The next 24 hours were spent in a flurry of ac-tivity in Douala. We had been warned to look out for muggers so we carried our passports, tickets and money in 'tubi-grip' elastic bandages on our legs. These are an excellent way of hiding valuables but they do have the drawback of becoming rather sweaty in tropical conditions! Douala is not the most exciting African city. It does not have the glamour of Nairobi, or the ex-travagance of Lagos or Cairo. Its streets are wide and rather characterless. Up-market restaurants and fashion houses give the place a much-needed splash of colour, but on the whole the dominant note is of business and little else.

The one feature of Douala that did impress us was the rain. When it comes down, it really pours. The entire population flees the streets in search of cover. Cars veer wildly along the roads, their drivers unable to see through the windscreen even with the wipers at high speed. The gutters immediately become torrents of floodwater and lakes form at junctions which are not adequately drained. Douala in summer is the city of a million umbrellas. Before leaving we bought supplies for our trip to Mount Cameroon. Our shopping list included choco-late, nuts, tinned fruit, vegetables, tea, coffee and sugar.

We then found a bush taxi for the journey out to Buea (pronounced 'Boy-a'). Mount Cameroon is situated conveniently near to Douala, and the journey time is only a couple of hours even in the slowest bus. Buea is the perfect base to use for walks on the mountain and has a fascinating history. When Bismark joined the scramble for Africa in 1883–1885 he declared Cameroon a German protectorate. Buea, with its cool climate and easily defended position, was chosen as the capital. The buildings of the

For hours the path continued steeply up through high tropical grass.

German colonial period can still be seen in the town. Nowadays, Buea has to be content with being the headquarters of the South-West Province, one of 10 which make up the Republic of Cameroon.

The taxi climbed gradually up the approach road to Buea, which sits at about 4,920ft (1.5km) above sea level. On either side of the road were the commercial enterprises of the town. The 'California Hair Salon' was one, '5 minute puncture repair' another. The one thing that did not seem to be sold was wellington boots, an odd omission in a town that was wallowing ankle-deep in glutinous mud. On the left-hand side as we came into Buea we found the tourist office. It was shut, but a strongly worded notice put the record straight. Anyone caught climbing Mount Cameroon, it informed readers, without a permit and guide from this office would be subject to a fine of 40,000 CFA and one-month imprisonment.

Ahead of us, for the first time, the mists parted and we had a fleeting glimpse of the upper flanks of the mountain. Like the Ruwenzori of east

Africa, Mount Cameroon spends much of the year shrouded in cloud. According to the *World Weather Guide*, 'A small area of Cameroon Peak is one of the three places in the world experiencing an average annual rainfall in excess of 400ins (10,000mm)! The other places are in the Hawaiian Islands and Assam in India.'

The mountain is 13,352ft (4,070m) high, making it the highest peak in tropical west Africa. It lies at the south-west end of a long string of volcanic mountains which constitute the border between Cameroon and Nigeria. These mountains are, from the north downwards, the Mandara, Shebshi, Adamawa highlands, Bamenda highlands, and finally the Mount Cameroon region. The Niger delta lies a short distance to the west. The island of Bioko (formerly known as Fernando Po) lies not many miles offshore with a high peak of 10,104ft (3,080m), an extension of the same range that gave birth to Mount Cameroon.

As night fell we checked into the Buea Mountain Hotel. It must once have been quite grand, but those days have long gone. A welcoming mosaic bearing the legend 'The Mountain Hotel' was cracked and soiled, the external window of the reception was missing, tropical creepers smothered the walls and the corrugated iron roofing was slowly oxidizing to rust. The room had the musty smell so typical of the tropics where nothing ever quite dries. The bedcovers were candlewick in faded green, and were embroidered 'Buea Mountain Hotel 1960'. That made them 30 years old! The sheets had no identifying dates on them but I think they might predate even the veteran bedcovers. The bathroom was equipped with ancient British sanitary ware, possibly from the late 1940s. Over the bath was installed a boiler which looked sufficiently powerful to propel a medium-size oil tanker, yet when asked to perform it reluctantly dribbled a pathetic flow of tepid water. By the time I came to bathe it was cold.

In the lounge, all the echoes of an illustrious past were collected in a wonderful array. The centrepiece of the room was a carved wooden fireplace with a homely open fire glowing for the benefit of the guests. Since we seemed the only ones we promptly took prime position. In the corner of the room was a folded-up ping-pong table. Above the fire was a huge polished mask with a yellowing elephant tusk beneath. A mirror sign informed the reader that 'Guinness is good for you', so we ordered two from the bar.

Various trophies were hung on the high walls. Black with age, they looked like a mixture of buffalo and antelope. Above the sideboard was a painting which provided us with the only clear view we were going to get of Mount Cameroon. The painting took as its point of view the scene from the gardens of the hotel. In the foreground it showed the swimming pool, packed with bathers. Behind them was the low-lying building of the hotel itself, and behind that, rising in a great conical mass, was Mount Cameroon. The lower slopes were picked out in dense tropical rainforest. The upper slopes were portrayed as grassy and devoid of vegetation.

The barman apologized that the hotel was so empty but we had arrived out-of-season. When we told him we were planning to climb the mountain he shuddered in horror: 'In the rains? You are mad!' and he had a point. It was at that very minute cascading down with incredible force. 'You will see' he continued, 'it is very cold up there! Much too cold!' Suddenly, sitting by that warm open fire, the thought of climbing thousands of feet up a rainy swamp was not so appealing. He continued to explain that the Guinness Mountain Marathon had now become an annual event every January, consisting of an international field of several hundred runners who gather in Buea for the race.

A more gruelling test of endurance would be hard to imagine. Not only is there the rigorous climb itself but the runners also face problems from high altitude and heat. Falls are common on the slippery downhill return. Incredibly, the record for the round trip to the summit and back now stands at under five hours. That makes an average of a vertical 2,000ft (610m) ascended and descended every hour! Some of the racers have adopted a curious practice which gives them a speed advantage on the descent. Taking a couple of long poles, they use them to launch themselves downhill. When this works they land 20–30ft (6–9m) further down the mountain having a nice soft landing on grass or the loose volcanic scree that covers the upper slopes. When it does not work, they crash down the slope at incredible velocity into something a good deal harder. Broken legs are not unknown in this peculiar race.

Our first task was to find a good guide. The receptionist at the Mountain Hotel spread the word in town and later that evening we met Nicholas to discuss our plans. He had the look of a mountain man about him, lean, wiry, and with 28 years' experience climbing Mount Cameroon. He looked at us with big, curiously sorrowful eyes. 'You know it will be very wet.' We told him we lived in a country where it rained a lot but he was not very impressed. 'Now is not a good time to be going up,' he went on. 'I was up last week and it was not good.' All of this, of course, was the preamble to the inevitable financial discussion which would follow. It emerged that there was a 'dry-season' rate and a 'wet-season' rate. The latter was incredibly high, even for a country recently named in a survey as one of the most expensive in the world. Nicholas wrote his opening figure on a piece of paper and passed it to me. It was so incredibly high that for a moment I thought he was giving me his telephone number. The evening wore on as we bargained him down to a more realistic figure. Eventually a deal was struck to the satisfaction of both sides and Nicholas departed into the rain-sodden night with a promise to meet us at 6 a.m. the following morning for the start of our trek.

At 6.30 a.m. we began the climb. This is the most humid part of the day with humidity levels commonly reaching 96 per cent in summer. Within a few minutes every shred of clothing was drenched, even though it was not raining. Nicholas was perfectly dry. Not a drop of sweat ran across his brow whereas Kees and I were running with perspiration. Anticipating wet foliage during the first part of the climb, I was wearing a pair of waterproof trousers. Kees found these highly amusing for their only effect was to make me twice as wet. Inside them, a layer of air collected which was being heated to furnace temperature. Humidity in there must have been 100 per cent. I stubbornly refused to admit they were a failure and stumbled on with my legs roasting away and rivers of sweat flowing out of the bottom.

For an hour we panted up a gently rising track which followed a course through semi-cultivated land. Nicholas stopped to poach a few head of corn from a plantation and popped them in his old 'rucksack' which had two shoulder straps ingeniously sown on. We were still in the layer of cloud that had shrouded Buea earlier on, but

The wet slopes of Mount Cameroon.

it was getting noticeably thinner as we continued the ascent. The path was well-defined and Nicholas hummed gently to himself as he led us up. Suddenly, the cultivated patches were left behind and we entered the twilight world of high-altitude rainforest. No sun could filter through the canopy here, it was thick and inpenetrable. The path continued to climb, a little steeper now, taking detours around giant trees. Some of their roots were as thick as any tree you can see in an English wood.

Without the path this vegetation would prove almost impossible to penetrate. It forms a wall of greenery, consisting of snagging tendrils and clutching thorns. Creepers hang from the higher branches and then become victim to other parasitic plants near the forest floor. Every living thing seems on a distorted, gigantic scale. One plant had leaves which were the size of dustbin lids. From every leaf drips a steady flow

97

Rain forest on Mount Cameroon – Humidity can reach 97 per cent.
(Photograph by Kees 't Hooft.)

of moisture culled from the water-rich air. And from the ground came a rich, peaty smell, the aroma of vegetation in the process of decay.

There had been no opportunity for breakfast before our departure that morning so we stopped after a couple of hours for bread and chocolate. We were both aware of the dangers of dehydration under these conditions and made sure we drank about 1½pts (1L) each. Nicholas drank nothing, being perfectly acclimatized to the conditions. To my amazement the tiny crumbs of bread which dropped on to the forest floor were almost immediately detected and cleared up by large black ants. Shortly after breakfast we came to the first hut. The mountain huts on Mount Cameroon are sturdily built, have no guardians, and are free to use. Nicholas said they were originally built by the Germans but were

now maintained by the prison department in Buea. This hut nestled in a small clearing in the rainforest and had an earthen floor. It was covered in graffiti and contained an assortment of firewood. Next to it was another, newer hut, which was raised on concrete legs above the floor. The ceilings of both buildings were stained jet black with soot.

In 1895 when Mary Kingsley climbed Mount Cameroon there were no huts for shelter. In fact very few people had then made the climb at all. It was a well-known peak to anyone who sailed around the coast of west Africa, but few of those early navigators felt the urge to climb it. Mary Kingsley did, despite admitting that she had little cause to go up mountains. Her ascent was predictably packed with incidents. There were porters who refused to go further, camps washed away by storms, attacks by swarms of bees, and casualties laid up for days with fevers and 'hot foot'. Travelling in Africa in the latter part of the nineteenth century was a difficult business, especially for a European woman. Eventually, after days of incredible hardship, Mary Kingsley made it to the top and left her calling card there. She was the first person to climb the mountain from the south-east, and one of the first women to have made the summit at all. Her account of the climb can be found in *Travels in West Africa*. It is a remarkable testimony to her courage that she succeeded, and there is no doubt that the profile of the mountain is raised every time a reader opens her book.

Close to the first hut is the only spring on the normal route up from Buea. It is surprising on a mountain which is the third rainiest place on earth that there are so few sources of running water. When it rains, the whole mountain is a network of torrents but these almost immediately soak into the band of thick rainforest in the foothills. We resupplied our water bottles at this source and drank as much as we could. Above, at hut number 2 there would be rainwater collected in barrels. Hut three and the route to the summit were dry.

The climb resumed through the rainforest. It was noticeably cooler now and we were sweating less. Chattering birds could be heard on all sides but we rarely saw them. Nicholas stopped a couple of times and said he could hear monkeys. They sounded like birds to us but he was the expert. Although we crept stealthily towards the sounds, we saw nothing. Suddenly, the path rose steeply up a bank and we were out of the rainforest. The dividing line between rainforest and grassland was dramatic. For the past few hours we had been unable to see more than a short distance in any direction, and there was no question of a view. Now, we were moving into wide open space, with clear drops down to the foothills and Buea. The cloud moved aside just at the right moment to reveal the

town. It looked a lot nearer than we had imagined it to be. Our hard work had not really gained us a great deal of height. Looking along the flank of the mountain we could see it rise in a uniform sweep. Regular eroded gullies swept downwards at intervals and were invaded by more of the rainforest that had been so successful lower down. Far away to the west we could just make out the flank of the outlying peak of Little Mount Cameroon and, beyond that, the sea. Nicholas pointed out the direction of Bioko island but the cloud was too dense to see it.

'This is the steepest part of the climb' said Nicholas, setting off up the slope. The path was marked with painted white rocks which would lead us to hut number 2. Enjoying the fresh breeze which played around the slope, we followed him at a steady plod. We were sandwiched in between two layers of cloud. Looking down we could see wispy drifts of cloud weaving in and out of the higher trees. There was something hypnotic about watching this happening. It was like observing an earlier chapter in the history of the earth, the rainforest a closed and secret world, locked under a blanket of grey-white vapour.

We caught up with Nicholas who was sitting beneath a lonely tree. His head was cradled in his hands and he looked thoroughly miserable. On the tree someone had nailed a tin sign 'Guinness is good for you'. 'I am tired' said Nicholas 'so very tired. I do not know why it should be so.' I wondered if it was too many Guinnesses the night before but 'No' he said, 'I don't drink. Never. You will never find me in a bar!' Thunder rolled in the direction of the sea, so we shouldered the packs and continued upwards. A couple of rises were gained and then the ground eased off providing a gentle rolling walk. Miniature trees had found a footing here, and Nicholas gathered dead branches for firewood as we went.

A few grassland birds were visible, including

99

*Guinness is good for you . . . even at hut
number 3 on Mount Cameroon!*

the stonechat with its distinctive 'wee-tuc-tuc'
call. Nicholas spotted the tracks of an antelope
in the muddy trail and declared them fresh. Of
the antelope itself, there was no sign. Around
the next bend lay hut number 2. It is quite a
large building situated at 9,350ft (2,850m). Most
of the space is taken up with a communal sleeping area and a separate hut is supposed to be for
cooking. In reality the sleeping areas are used for
both functions. Nicholas chose a small annexe
on the end of the main hut for our base. It was
slightly less squalid than the other hut, and
more light filtered in through the door. A
wooden sleeping platform had been constructed
at the rear of the room and large pile of firewood
lay near the door. It was the perfect base, or so
we thought.

Nicholas dusted down some of the foam mat-
tresses that littered the floor and we sat down for
a rest. He lit a fire and we made up soup and tea.
The hut soon filled with choking smoke which
made the eyes water. It was just past midday. We
had been walking for nearly six hours and
gained about 4,429ft (1,350m) in height. Quite

a lot of the time had been devoted to gaining
horizontal distance in the rainforest. I went on
a recce to see what the water situation was like.
The supply was held in two rusty oil drums
positioned under the cut-off drainpipes of the
roof. The first was dirty and polluted with bird
droppings but the second, protected more by the
slant of the tin roof, looked fairly clean. I filled
our water bottles and added a couple of drops of
iodine as a precaution.

We now had to make a decision about our tac-
tics for the rest of the climb. We could continue
up to hut three but we knew there was no water
there. We could stay for the afternoon and night
at hut two and go for an early morning bash up
to the summit and return the same day. Or we
could leave the packs at hut two and carry on
straight away to the summit, returning there for
the night before descending the next day. It
largely depended on the rain. So far we had been
very lucky. Nicholas went outside and tested the
air with a stalk of grass. 'This afternoon' he announced, 'it will not rain.' I asked Kees his
opinion. He preferred to keep going while the
weather held. I agreed. Nicholas had got over
his tired streak with the aid of six teaspoonfuls of
sugar in his coffee. We were perfectly placed for
a summit bid.

In thick cloud we left the hut and followed the
path up an attractive defile where large trees
dotted the landscape. They looked like the last
remnants of a great forest. Sadly, a great many of
them seemed to be dying, or dead, and their
proximity to hut two is a problem. In winter trekkers must consume a lot of firewood from these
trees. Deforestation in general seems to be rapid
on Mount Cameroon. Even Mary Kingsley's
account of the climb only 100 years before gives
the impression of far more forest than is currently
the case. Leaving the trees behind, we started
another steep grassy section. A phantom rock
painter had clearly keen enjoying himself in this
area. White rocks marking the route were
evident every few yards. It seemed excessive

Approaching hut number 3.

until really thick cloud rolled in and severely reduced visibility. Then, the white rocks were the only way to keep on the right track.

Carrying only water, chocolate and raingear we could move much faster than before. Within an hour we were looking down on the shiny roof of hut two. The weather continued to threaten rain and we could hear the sound of thunder. Buea was now a very long way off. It was revealed by sporadic gaps in the cloud, a thin scattering of habitation surrounded by solid green. The steep section lasted for perhaps 2,000ft (610m) and then eased off into scooped-out gullies which looked like the spill-off from a gravel quarry. The rock became more noticeably volcanic in nature, and the grass cover began to thin out. Half an hour later we rounded a lump and discovered hut three.

Positioned at 12,467ft (3,800m), hut number 3 is just high enough to detect the effects of high altitude. Fortunately the amount of graffiti on the hut is noticeably less than on the previous two. Either people run out of puff before they get

here . . . or their aerosols do not work at this height! We shared out the last few squares of chocolate and then set off for the last scramble for the summit. Now we began to leave the clouds behind. For the first time we found ourselves walking in sunlight. The character of the mountain had now completely changed. Only odd tussocks of grass found a footing in the volcanic ash. The path coursed up, getting progressively more dusty and arid as it went.

It would have been a beautiful climax to the climb but it was getting harder to ignore the plastic water bottles and other rubbish that was scattered on the ground. Most of the litter is the result of the Guinness marathon. The runners gulp down 1½pts (1L) in one go and chuck away the bottles. The organizers ought to clear up the mess but they do not. At last, we emerged at the saddle which marks the edge of the crater. Nicholas told us that the last eruption had been in 1956 but we could see no sign of activity in the form of smoke or fumes. It was hard to imagine that this was a live volcano. Shortly after, we skirted around an incline and gained the summit. Nicholas gave a touching little speech about our climb, and about how the gods had smiled on us and kept off the rain.

Someone had placed an army ammunition box at the top for people to put their comments in. The last message was just three weeks old. The writer was Steve from Harrogate, Yorkshire. So we were not the only people mad enough to climb Cameroon in the rainy season! The rest were mostly by French and Italians. Many portrayed their struggles to reach the summit in graphic terms. 'Took everything I've got to get here', was one. 'Nearly killed me!' was another. If we had come for the view, we were to be disappointed. Our minutes on the summit were spent in dense cloud. Then it began to spit with a few drops of rain and Nicholas urged us to descend. We had just enough time to get back down to hut two before dark. We scribbled our names in the book and left.

The summit of Mount Cameroon. A 'visitors' book' is contained within a metal box for suitable comments.

Hut number 2, Mount Cameroon. Watch out for the rats!

Back at the hut Nicholas lit a fire to cook supper. He roasted the corn he had picked on the way up and we ate it hungrily. More nourishment came from cans of peas and noodles. We crawled into our sleeping bags on the sleeping platform and only then found out the disadvantage of hut two – rats. The place was alive with them. They scampered over our sleeping bags, scratched at our rucksacks, and nosed about in the empty cans on the floor. Kees woke up to find one eating bread just inches away from his head. He shone his torch directly at the rodent but it just kept on nibbling as if to say 'Oh, decent of you to put some light on the scene!' He chased it away and built a tower of boots and other equipment with the bread on top. Five minutes later the rat was back on top of the tower. Kees admired this endeavour and gave up chasing them away. I was less keen and eventually slept outside. I preferred to get wet.

In the morning we prepared to descend to Buea. We intended to take our time and explore some more of the rainforest on the lower slopes. After breakfast we packed up the gear. Nicholas took the remainder of our bread, broke it up and scattered the pieces around the hut. 'What are you doing that for?' I asked 'For the rats!' he replied. Kees said, 'You know, in Europe we would put down poison.' Nicholas turned to him in delight: 'Aha! That is a comment on the state of the world! Only in Africa would the people put down bread!' It was a homespun piece of philosophy which had all three of us doubled up with laughter. We started the descent to Buea, leaving the rats of hut number 2 to their meal.

The Mandara

Tucked away in the northernmost extremity of Cameroon are a range of mountains called Mandara. They are typical of many such ranges in Africa. Hidden away in an obscure corner, not possessing any peaks likely to attract attention, they lie largely ignored. Yet, like all 'secret' ranges, the rewards of walking through the Mandara are rich. I, for one, cannot resist the lure of mountains whose name is known to so few.

The Mandara are contained within the slender finger of Cameroonian land which stretches up to Lake Chad. So narrow is this corridor, with Chad to one side and Nigeria on the other, that you are left in no doubt as to the importance of reaching the lake. Thus, the Mandara form the

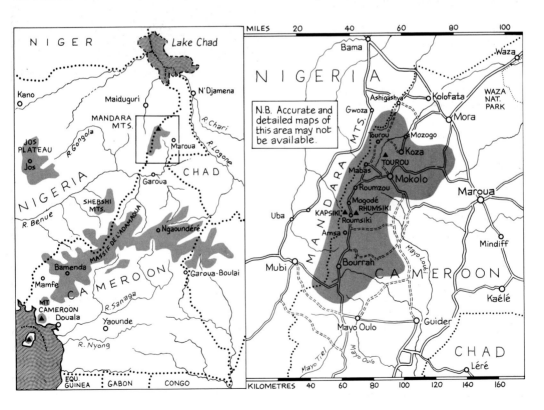

effective natural border on the Nigerian side, whilst on the Chadian side this role falls to the Logone River. The Mandara has its southern-most extension in the regions of Mayo-Tsanaga, and to the north at the Parc National de Mozogo-Gokoro. The heart of the Mandara, and the area which was the focus of my own journey, is the area to the south-west of Mokolo, and in particular, the village of Rhoumsiki. With me was Kees 't Hooft, my companion up Mount Cameroon.

At Maroua we arranged a bush taxi for the 50-mile (80km) drive to Mokolo. Monsieur Hassini, the driver, set off at a fair pace and then stopped beside a muddy pool. His next actions mystified us. First, he took a handful of glutinous, stinking mud. Then he started to plaster it on the side of the taxi with elaborate care. We asked why. 'It's a precaution,' he told us, 'against the police. I always do it when I leave the town.' His handiwork was well done. After finishing, the number of his taxi was completely obscured and we were travelling incognito. How the police at the frequent roadblocks ever fell for this rudimentary trick was beyond imagination. But they did, and we passed through with no problems.

At Mokolo we refuelled from one of the many roadside vendors who sell petrol and diesel by the litre in old mineral water bottles. The fuel is apparently smuggled from Nigeria. So keen were the two boys who carried out the refuelling exercise that they splashed large quantities on the ground. Even larger quantities splashed over them but they did not seem to mind! Monsieur Hassini negotiated a suitable reduction for spillage and we continued. The good tarmac road vanished as we started the 30-mile (48km) 'piste' to Rhoumsiki. It was the middle of the rainy season and the track was only just passable for a two-wheel drive vehicle. Monsieur Hassini drove with care, wincing in anguish every time a protruding rock scraped the belly of his taxi. Luckily it had not rained that day so we were able to forge the rivers that ran across the road.

The Mandara began to make themselves felt as we continued south just a few miles from the Nigerian border. A profusion of boulders and rocks was scattered about the landscape. Opportunist patches of cultivation were dotted between them in irregularly shaped plots. Maize and groundnuts were the main crops. Brightly clad figures could be seen working in the fields. Just visible above the maize were the elegant conical roofs of local compounds. The huts are mostly circular and finely constructed of stone with a tough infill of mud dried to the hardness of cement. Approximately 6–10 of these palm-topped huts are clustered together within a compound wall 6ft (1.8m) high. The end result is visually appealing – a picture-book African village, completely different from the half-built shanty towns further south in Cameroon.

Although the collections of huts resemble tiny villages, in reality they are the compounds of extended families. Subdivisions of the area provide stabling for goats and cattle, the latter being magnificent in the Mandara region. Grazing is good in the rains, and the Zebu herds looked sleek and well-fed. Some of the mature specimens had horns a full 6ft (1.8m) from tip to tip. These are the pride and joy of their owners and the subjects of many complicated rituals and beliefs. Not only in India is the cow considered sacred.

Children waved happily to us as Monsieur Hassini continued his painstaking drive. Women with children on their backs, stopped work in the fields and smiled. In the late afternoon sun the Mandara looked lush and green. The broad sweeping valleys turned up dramatically at the edges where piles of gigantic volcanic rocks lay stacked tidily on top of each other. In the midst of this calm and fertile scenery, it was hard to imagine that just to the east lay war-torn Chad, currently one of the poorest and least stable countries in the African continent. And it is still harder to remember that not far to the north was the drought zone of the Sahel belt. The Mandara is increasingly a refuge for people from those less fortunate regions.

Suddenly, Kees let out a yell and Monsieur Hassini stopped abruptly. The cause was a smallish bird sitting on the high point of a clump of elephant grass next to the road. Its colours were so startlingly bright that at first I mistook it for a sweet wrapper or piece of cloth tied to the grass. Then it flew off with a low fluttering flight and revealed an impossibly rich plumage of vivid red. We consulted the Collins *Field Guide to the Birds of West Africa* and discovered that it was a Fire-Crowned Bishop (*Euplectes hordeaceus*). Even the colour picture could not do the bird justice — I have never before seen such a brilliant scarlet.

Gradually the scenery grew even more impressive. Whereas it had previously been rolling and unobtrusive, now volcanic plugs began to loom on the horizon. The valleys became more deeply cut, the sides punctuated by exposed faces and rocky walls. We were travelling on a high plateau, with fewer villages and compounds visible. Several hundred feet below a stream could just be picked out, a silver-white line running through low-lying green shrubs and bush.

At Rhoumsiki the full splendour of the Mandara is revealed. Lofty skyscrapers of sheer rock compete for attention on every side. To the west the mountains peel away in jagged confusion towards the Nigerian border. It is not hard to think oneself back a few million years to a time when this was a bubbling cauldron of volcanic activity. The tall volcanic plugs are all that remain of the cores that once filled the vents of the Mandara's volcanoes. Erosion rates are extremely fast in regions subjected to a season of tropical rains and the softer ash and debris which surrounded the plugs has long been washed away.

At the village we found accommodation in a small 'campement'. A stuffed python had been

The beautiful valley at Rhoumsiki.

hung at an erratic angle on the wall next to various masks and raffia fetish items. Whichever way you looked at the unfortunate snake, it was impossible to tell which end was which. Presumably, the poor beast had been decapitated for good measure when captured. The patron opened two beers with a flourish of the bottle opener. Cameroon has excellent breweries and even the smallest bar manages to produce its wares in ice-cool condition. We told the patron that we were planning to go walking in the area and asked him if we could find a guide. As usual, we had no decent maps of the region so a guide was essential.

The word went out and a couple of guides turned up. The first was obviously drunk and did not exude enthusiasm for the task ahead. The second, Alex, was a much younger man and seemed fitter. He told me that he had been a guide for 15 years and that he was 18 years old. When I pointed out that this had him guiding and backpacking at the age of three, he was not in the least put out. 'We start early here' he assured us, 'as a trainee guide.' We settled on a price after some tough haggling on both sides.

There was just time for a quick scramble up the cluster of rocks that cast a shadow over the village. We followed Alex's barefoot figure up the steep climb and were rewarded by a breathtaking sunset. Below us the chatter of playing children and the comforting sounds of animals filtered up through windless air. The valley of Rhoumsiki was quiet and still, resembling timeless scenes one sees in engravings from the books of early African explorers. On the return we bought provisions for the walk. Rice, sugar, tea and coffee were the staples. Oil, onions, tomatoes and maize were the luxuries. Alex

assured us we would be able to buy chickens in the villages if we felt the need for meat. We debated whether to take beer but decided against it on grounds of weight, our packs were already heavy enough.

By the light of a crescent moon we sat on the terrace of the campement and downed a number of beers. The ghostly shadows of the greater plugs could just be traced on the valley floor. Crickets and cicadas rasped their lovesongs from every bush and dogs barked at each other in the village. A Toyota Landcruiser turned up and a group of travel-weary VIPs joined us for a drink. They were the Ambassadors of Israel and Belgium on an upcountry tour with their families. With the help of more beer and a carafe of distinctly rugged Cameroonian wine, the evening turned into a lively social event. The Israeli Ambassador and his wife treated us to a firecracker display of wit which would have shamed most professional comedy double-acts

Village in the Mandara Mountains, northern Cameroon.

into retiring. The Belgian Ambassador told us some wonderfully indiscreet tales about diplomatic life and only fear of provoking an international incident prevents me from retelling them here!

When the bar ran out of beer we crawled off to bed. It was much, much, too late to be retiring, with our 5 a.m. deadline for departure only a few hours off. 'That wine was a mistake' groaned Kees, as his first movements of the day were thwarted by an aching head. I could only agree. We lit the camping stove to brew tea, and sat in the darkness of the African night, wondering if we really wanted to walk that day. With slow, ponderous actions, the rucksacks were packed. We were taking food, stove, spare clothes, raingear for the inevitable storms, sleeping bag, mosquito net, karrimats, and camera gear. We had water bottles to carry only 5pts (3L) each as we knew we could get water from the villages.

As first light filtered through the trees of the campement, Alex turned up. He was carrying his gear for the walk in a sports bag which had four castor wheels on the base and was wearing a Cameroonian football team supporter's shirt. We set off up the main, indeed, only, street in Rhoumsiki, just as the village was coming to life. Most African mountain guides consider that speed is the sign of a job well done and start off at an incredible velocity. Alex was no exception. His rate was about that of the average trot, carried out with a curious gliding stride which reminded me of someone trying to go langlaufing but without skis.

He soon realized that we were no match for this speed and dropped back to our more gentle plodding progress. A small boy latched on to our tail as we left Rhoumsiki behind. For a few miles we followed the southern road from the village. This eventually ends up at Garoua 124 miles (200km) later, but is generally considered impassable in the rainy season for vehicles. In the cool of the early morning people were already busy at their work in the fields. Next to each worker was an enamel bowl or gourd containing manioc or maize meals — sustaining food is essential if you are to spend the day working the land. Several fields were being put to the plough. This, unlike the more menial jobs of planting, tending and weeding, is obviously man's work. Despite the high numbers of cattle in the region the only animals we saw yoked for ploughing were donkeys.

Leaving the track to the east, we set off across country along a winding path. The young boy, an urchin dressed in a ripped velveteen shirt and a ragged pair of shorts, was still following. Alex stopped and shouted at him to go back, but he stayed with us, padding silently behind at a distance of 150ft. Alex began to get annoyed. We did not need a translator to know that he was threatening the boy. Yet he still followed us. At last Alex lost his temper and, turning suddenly, chased the boy back towards Rhoumsiki. The boy, perhaps fearing for his life, outran Alex easily. Perhaps following in this way is the apprenticeship of a trainee guide. One hour later, when we looked behind, the little brat was still there, 150ft behind, grinning like an idiot!

The plain we were walking across was gently undulating, and carpeted with grass and wild flowers. The thatched hut compounds were hidden behind walls which were decorated on top with gourds and broken pottery. A blackheaded heron flew off as we approached. Not only was it easy to identify the bird from our west Africa field guide, but there was a wealth of other information as well. The heron was, we learned, 'partial to open grassy or cultivated ground in the savanna, including the Cameroon highlands'. The amount of research involved in the work, and the superb illustrations, make this a valuable asset when walking in Africa. Even if, like me, you are not a keen birdwatcher, there is an undeniable pleasure in being able to identify birds in the field.

The sun rose relentlessly in a blue sky until

just after 9 a.m., when clouds appeared and we were shaded from the heat. Thunder drummed away ominously to the north but we saw no sign of rain. Meanwhile each of us carried on our backs, and hats, up to 100 'hitchhiking' flies. When we stopped or broke rhythm they would buzz around in irritating droves. Why flies hitchhike like this has always mystified me. Do they like the feeling of movement? Do they know there will be a tasty meal of sweat every time the innocent victim stops for a rest? Or do they perhaps feel like a change of scenery without being bothered to fly. By late morning we came to a river. Kees and I sat beneath an old tree while Alex went to find a contact in the nearby village. As if by magic, as soon as he had gone, we were surrounded by small children who materialized from nowhere. There was no sign of our follower but he was probably hiding in the bush.

Alex came back and explained that we must wait in the village for the chief to return. Only by paying our respects to the chief would we be allowed to continue to the next village. He would, Alex assured us, send one of his sons with us to act as our passport to the next chief's territory. This is a common feature of travelling in remote rural parts of Africa and gives the bush telegraph a chance to send news that strangers are coming through. While we were waiting, he asked, would we like to see the local blacksmith in action? Of course. Off we went through fields of maize to the compound of a 'forgeron'. He was a dignified old man with Fulani style robes and eyes which looked as if they were perpetually squinting against the smoke of the fire. The heat was bouncing off the mud walls of the compound and Kees and I were in need of a drink. We waited a decent interval to see if one would be offered but, when nothing happened, brewed up tea which Alex and the 'forgeron' drank with us.

It was fascinating to see inside a compound. The thatched conical roofs were even more intricate seen close up than they appeared at a distance. The stones forming the hut walls were well-dressed and laid. Separate, smaller circular huts contained goats and chickens. The sleeping quarters of the smith were little more than a couple of blankets laid on the earthen floor. Some enamel pots and pans lay in neat piles next to a washing bowl. A few chairs were brought to us in our honour and the smith prepared to give us a demonstration of his art. First he cut up pieces of wood of just the right size for the task in hand. Then he lit a small fire and tended it lovingly until he had a substantial bed of red-hot coals. All the while smoke constantly blew up into the smith's face, yet he hardly seemed to notice. We sat hypnotized by the languid ceremony. Even though we were impatient to get up into the mountains, this demonstration had a charm which was hard to resist.

A large metal tray was produced and the coals were placed on it. The smith used his hands as one would use a pair of tongs. So thick was his skin that he could lift even the hottest pieces of wood from the fire to the tray. He then explained the process by which the metal objects were cast. He had one ready for firing, a small metal jug made from wound copper. He sealed a cast with clay and water. To our surprise, he then left the compound and walked us through more fields until we reached the forge, a beehive-shaped clay and rock structure. It stood on its own, far from any buildings and surrounded by the shards of broken clay from previous firings. I wondered if, as is the case in many societies, the forge was the subject of powerful taboos. Certainly smiths and their families are subjected to a great many unique rules governing what they can and cannot do within the community.

The smith then carefully placed the coals and fresh wood in the forge and attached two soft leather bellows to two indented depressions. These connected by underground channel to the forge where the air pumped into the fire. Taking the bellows in each hand the smith

'Forgeron' in the Mandara Mountains.

'When the forgeron is dead' Alex said, with little concern whether the old chap overheard, 'this son will continue his work.' Meanwhile the son fetched a metal urn which contained water. The smith took one last look inside the forge and took out the cast, clutched between the pincers of an ancient pair of tongs. He tested its temperature by holding strands of grass against it to see how well they burned. Then, with a grand gesture, he plunged the cast into the metal pot with a satisfying hiss. Soon, the cast was cool enough to handle and the smith chipped off the blackened clay to reveal the gleaming metal jug beneath. We burst into a round of spontaneous applause. It was a masterful performance — a real piece of theatre.

Gathering together the equipment we returned to the compound and examined the jug and some of the other items that the smith was fond of making. There were bracelets and charms and knives. As a gesture of thanks we made him a small gift of money through Alex, who then gave a touching vote of thanks from the smith. Outside the compound, we saw the child who had been following us yet again! He was hiding in a patch of prickly pear, smiling that idiotic smile and prepared to run for his life if Alex turned on him. In fact Alex ignored him. Perhaps it would have been undignified to chase him in front of the smith. Or perhaps Alex was warming to the advances of his aspiring assistant. Either way, the boy seemed well pleased to be with us. Hidden in the maize he had obviously been watching the smith's performance.

Although we had been expecting to see the chief, and meet his son, neither appeared. So the smith suggested that his son accompany us to the next village, called Amsa. Since we were keen to get on with our walk we readily agreed. The next couple of hours passed in a haze of heat. We were constantly drinking from the water bottles to restore our moisture loss through sweat. Even Alex, carrying a far lighter load than us, was dripping. The plain rolled on

began a pulsating and rhythmical performance. He varied the beat depending on the state of the glowing fire in the forge. When it waned he would up the frequency of the bellows. When it roared he would ease off a little. Kees sat transfixed, watching with rapt attention the hands of the smith as they pummelled the bellows. Every few minutes the smith took a stick and poked about in the forge to survey the state of the clay cast he had put inside. It was glowing almost white-hot. He went on pumping, seeming to ignore the billowing clouds of white smoke which plumed continuously into his face. His son now appeared and loaded handfuls of fresh grass on to the fire. The smoke increased and the flame roared until the smith was almost obscured by cloud.

for a while and then we climbed a steady rise to a low shoulder where more mountains stretched before us. At last we were climbing into the real Mandara. We waded through a fast-flowing river and joined a well-trodden path heading south-west.

On each side were the thorn stockades of animal enclosures and the ever-present compounds. Judging from the reaction of the occupants as we passed, strangers were not frequent in these parts. About 15 miles (25km) into the Mandara it became more common to see women, particularly the elders, wearing nothing but a chain of beads around their waist. The beads supported two strategically placed sprigs of vegetation, fore and aft. There were few travellers on the path, just the occasional boy herding goats or women shouldering great loads of firewood, bent double by the weight.

Now we climbed another pass and entered a valley which was by far the most beautiful we had seen so far. A clear stream ran down its course, and water-washed boulders flanked the water. Small children splashed in a pool while the adults of the villages worked on the steep slopes above. Trees were more frequent here than in the lower valleys, offering occasional shade on the path. We stopped to eat and drink. The menu was not exactly to gourmet standard but the dried soup restored our salt levels and the sweet tea restored energy. The smith's son was still with us even though we had long since passed the village of Amsa. We had specifically asked Alex to take us to a remote area, high into the mountains, and now this was happening he was showing signs of anxiety. Privately, we decided that he was not totally sure where we were. The smith's son was much more certain. This was his home territory. People in the fields waved cheerful greetings to him even though we were at least 6 miles (10km) from his home.

The walk continued up the valley for the best part of an hour and then levelled off on to a flatter plain formed by the confluence of three

The Mandara mountains of northern Cameroon.

great spurs. A well filled with toads sat in the middle of what looked like a football pitch. There was, Alex told us, a great village ahead where we could possibly stay for the night which was a very welcome thought. We were getting quite tired after a whole day in the tropical African sun. Several times it looked as if it might rain but so far it had held off.

A small procession of cattle and donkeys came past us on the track. Alex took a fancy to a leather pouch owned by a small girl with the animals. After some bargaining he bought it. To my horror he paid for it in naira – the currency of Nigeria! 'Are we in Nigeria?' I asked him, knowing in these mountains how easy it would be to accidentally cross the border. He answered

'No' but we were not convinced. The prospect of being discovered by a Nigerian army patrol with no visa was not appealing. A large village came into sight. It was clearly a local market. An area for slaughtering livestock was stained with blood, and a collection of small hearths showed where traders roasted corn and meat. The day we arrived, however, nothing was happening, which gave the place a rather dismal feel.

Our follower was still with us, all the time getting closer and closer. Alex had by now adopted the policy of completely ignoring him . . . which the boy found very flattering. For a six- or seven-year-old he had now walked an extremely long way from home through alien lands. He obviously has a taste for adventure. Leaving the village behind we started a steep climb up a rocky track. The stream dried up after 30 minutes of ascent and we were now hotter than ever. In front of us lay the col. No, a false alarm. More climbing ahead. We did not have the energy to ask Alex how much further the climb would take us. It was better not to know. Now and then a light breeze blew up and gave us momentary relief. Then it was back to a humid upward slog. We were sweating pints.

At last our two guides pointed to a large collection of huts on two sides of the steep valley. Here the route narrowed, trees offered shade, and a source of water lay trapped in some rocks. Fifty paces further on we branched right into a field system and arrived in a compound. We flopped down on to the ground in two heaps, our shirts wrung through with sweat. The name of the village, said Alex, was Wralalla. It was not a place which gave us a good feeling. A couple of paces from where we sat was the spot used by children and animals as their toilet. Four or five ill-looking old men were lying listlessly in a domed hut. They showed no interest whatever in us, Alex, or the smith's son. No women were to be seen. The children were all heavily encrusted with weeping sores on their legs, each one ringed by a bracelet of hungry flies. Their bellies were distended with worms.

There was an indefinable feeling of hopelessness about the place. I got up and went to the hut. My efforts to greet the occupants were ignored. And then the smell within the hut finally permeated my nostrils. It was the smell of stale beer that finished me. The previous night's alcoholic excesses had been hard enough to ignore all day and Kees had been feeling very fragile that morning. Now, after the long hot climb on a virtually empty stomach, with the memories of last night's beers all too fresh, I came extremely close to fainting. I sat down on a wall. Blackness began to close in as my eyes began to go into tunnel vision. The smell of that rotten beer in the hut kept wafting over. The nausea mounted. My tongue swelled up as I heard myself saying, 'Kees, I think I'm going to faint.'

Luckily, Kees acted quickly and put me on the ground with my head between my legs. He brewed tea and we both drank about 2½pts (2L) of the precious liquid, boiling it up in relays on our small stove. After that I felt much better. Alex asked us if we wanted to wait for the chief to arrive. Then, he informed us, we might be able to stay in the village. That was absolutely the last thing on our minds. All we wanted was to get away from the place as fast as possible. This was not somewhere to stay, although we would have been hard pressed to describe exactly why. Other villages had been substantially the same yet we had felt perfectly at home in them. There we did not.

In a strange kind of way that experience reflected our dilemma. We did not know where we were going. We had no good maps. We had guides whose knowledge of the area was good, but their means of communicating information to us was slow and imprecise because of language differences. No wonder we had got to the stage where we stumbled into a village where we were not welcome. Yet, for myself, that is the way I

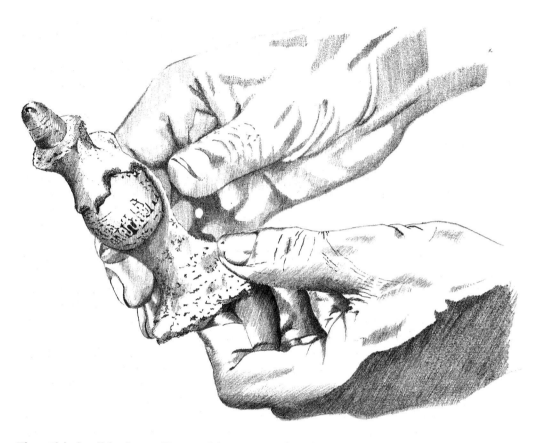

The smith broke off the clay mould to reveal the treasure inside.

prefer to explore a mountain range. Arrive unexpected and unannounced. Then you discover the real situation as the original explorers of Africa might have done. If you arrive in an organized group, you have the illusion of adventure. The mud huts will look the same. The villages will be equally interesting. But the people are expecting your arrival, and their response to you is predetermined. The way that Kees and I were travelling, anything could happen, good or bad. If offered, hospitality would be spontaneous. Hostility would be no less genuine. We were taking the rough with the smooth.

Shouldering the saturated backpacks we descended a north-facing route down the mountainside to a dry valley. If there had been water there we would have bivouaced out for the night and taken a risk on getting wet if it rained. As it was, we continued across an arid plateau towards some distant villages. Now, a small argument between Alex and the smith's son blew up. It seemed they did not know quite where to go next. We sat down on the sandy floor and waited as their discussion continued. Alex paused for a few moments to dig hurriedly at the ground. I thought he was digging a small rodent out of its burrow but in fact he produced a disc-shaped root which exuded a milky sap. It smelt like a turnip and Alex assured us it was good eating.

There was one hour to sunset and we had been walking almost solidly since 6 a.m. We were tired, thirsty, and in need of shelter. Could Alex deliver? The argument between the two men seemed to diminish when we reminded Alex that we were so close to nightfall. They led us off in a new direction, slightly more to the east, without saying why. Almost exactly one hour later we came to a compound protected with a tangled mass of prickly pear. Alex vanished inside and emerged a few moments later with the news that we were welcome to stay. The interior of the compound was spacious and well organized. Neatly stacked piles of firewood were placed in a methodical fashion along one wall. A mangy dog eyed us warily but the welcome from the inhabitants was warm. Monsieur Tagouva was the chief of this particular area, and he could not have been kinder in his reception of two tired and sweaty strangers straight out of the bush.

We gave him some of our rice and oil and he told his sons to catch a chicken. This was easier said than done, as the compound chickens ran wild in their attempts to avoid capture. Eventually two were caught and Alex was given the delicate job of deciding which one we should eat. The fatter of the two was chosen for the pot. Kees put on his head torch and began reading his Shackleton biography. I was happy to lie back and listen to the babble of conversation which surrounded us. It was still hot but an occasional breeze cooled us down.

The chicken arrived, steaming beneath a rich sauce and resting on a bed of rice. We were hungry for protein, and tore into the meat with relish. What a day it had been! Filled with the ups and downs of haphazard mountain travel, it had ended for the good. We had shelter for the night, we had food, we were amongst friends. What more could the Mandara give us? Neither of us knew what the next few days would contain. We would work our way through more of these beautiful mountains, never knowing what was around the corner. At the end we would return to Rhoumsiki and good beer. Which one of these two worlds is the real Cameroon? They both are.

I wandered out into the bush to brush my teeth before turning in for the night. The stars were exceptionally clear. On returning to the compound I noticed that Alex and the smith's son were already fast asleep underneath a blanket. Tucked into the same blanket was the tiny figure of the child who had followed us through the long hot walk. It had been a good day for him too.

Fact Sheets

ALGERIA

Getting There

Overland routes from Morocco and Tunisia are often used to get into Algeria although the Moroccan border has on occasion been shut due to the ongoing conflict between the two countries over the Western Saharan War. Seek advice on this from embassies and consulates before you go. From Europe, the main direct overland route is by ferry from the south of France. There are plenty of these running between Marseille and Algiers but they are not cheap. Regular flights from Europe connect Algiers and Oran to most major cities. Paris is, of course, the main hub but there are direct flights to London as well. I have never heard of charter flights going to Algeria.

Access to the Mountains

The Hoggar and Tassili both lie in the far south of Algeria, well into the central region of the Sahara desert. Travelling to them overland is an adventure in its own right, and not to be undertaken without considerable thought and planning. The so-called 'tarmac' road to Tamanrasset has lured many an unsuspecting traveller to disaster when attempted in a standard two-wheel drive car. The burned out wrecks on the 'piste' are enough to tell you that. If you do decide to travel down through Algeria into the Sahara you should seek out one of the excellent books which deal with the subject in more detail. *The Sahara Handbook* by Simon and Jan Glen is the best source for this.

Once at the oasis towns of Tamanrasset or Djanet, you are sufficiently near to the mountains to make the logistics manageable.

Street scene in Ghardaia, Algeria.

It is perfectly possible to fly into Tamanrasset or Djanet using connecting flights from Algiers. These are cheap and normally quite efficient. If you have only a limited time to spend in the mountains, this is really the best way to go about it. The office of Air Algérie in London will give you details of flights and prices.

Language

French and Arabic are the two most widely spoken languages in Algeria. You will find some people who speak excellent English but you will definitely need some French to get by with. Learning a few words of Arabic (numbers, greeting, etc.) is a really good idea.

Trekking Equipment

Ultra-lightweight trekking gear is the key to comfortable days in the central Sahara but have enough clothing with you to cope with freezing conditions at night. Protection from the burning rays of the sun is very important so take hats, goggles and plenty of loose clothing with which to cover up. A length of cloth for use as a turban will help against sandstorms and preserve moisture from the breath. Good boots with ankle protection are, as ever, essential.

Do not underestimate just how cold the nights can be. In winter, with a wind blowing, a high-quality sleeping bag will be essential. A bobble hat is a good idea and a down jacket is advisable. In summer, of course, daytime temperatures are incredibly high and the nights are pleasantly warm. No matter what sort of equipment you carry, walking in the Sahara in summer is going to be extreme. It is best to keep to the winter months unless you really are experienced in summer conditions and have acclimatized over several months to the prevailing conditions.

Water supplies are always unpredictable so carry enough plastic bottles to cover your needs. The expedition advisory centre of the Royal Geographical Society can supply charts showing water consumption under different conditions.

Seasons

The Sahara desert is one of the most extreme weather zones on Earth. The climate is virtually without rain, although some precipitation occurs during the summer months when violent storms spill over from the tropics. In the high mountains, such as the Hoggar, rain occurs more frequently, and the unique flash floods that run off these ranges should be treated with great caution. If you camp in a wadi, you may be swept away by a wall of torrential water, even though the rain has fallen many miles away. I have seen a dry wadi the width of the Thames at Hammersmith bridge fill up with 4 feet (1.2m) of water and then completely dry up again in one 24-hour period.

Other factors to bear in mind are the ferocious windstorms that blow sand and dust with enough velocity to strip the paint off a car and glaze the windscreen as if sandblasted.

The overriding factor if you consider walking in the Sahara is of course, heat. Exhaustion and dehydration are a very real danger if the correct procedures are not followed. Adequate water and salt intake is absolutely fundamental to maintain life in these conditions and a large supply of water should always be on hand for contingency if something should go wrong. Never travel alone in any season in the Sahara desert.

Temperatures of 50°C (120°F) are recorded in the months of July and August. Temperatures in the low twenties (°C) are more likely in winter. The police and immigration authorities of the countries which govern the Sahara sometimes restrict travel during the hottest months of the year. The winter months are really the only viable, and comfortable, months to travel in.

Medical

Your local doctor will advise on current innoculations for Algeria. Protection against heatstroke is essential. Good barrier creams for any exposed skin surfaces are advised, as are salt tablets and precautions against malaria.

Water, even from the most remote wells, should be boiled or purified before drinking. Food should be well cooked and from a trusted source. Seek expert advice from a tropical medicine hospital if you are interested in current advice on serums and antidotes for snakebite or scorpion.

115

Visas

British citizens do not currently need visas for Algeria but there are rumours that this may shortly change. Check on up-to-date requirements with your nearest Algerian Embassy.

Guides

In the Tassili plateau region you are required to have an official guide approved by the National Park Authority. This means you have to sign up for an official tour with one of the incredibly expensive travel agents which operate from the Oasis of Djanet, which is the base for all the trips. The only way to get this price down is to arrive there with enough time to wait for more travellers to come through and sign up. Or you can go on a prepaid package tour with a UK operator.

In the Hoggar, walking and camel trips are organized by the official Algerian tourist authority in Tamanrasset. People who go off alone are generally frowned upon, and I have even been told that walking without a guide in the Hoggar is now technically illegal. Enquire with the office in Tamanrasset and be prepared to wait for more travellers to turn up so that the collective price can go down. You may find likely candidates at the campsite.

CAMEROON

Getting There

Cameroon borders with Nigeria, Chad, Equatorial Guinea, Congo, Gabon and the Central African Republic. There are land routes across all of these into the country. From Europe there are regular air connections from Geneva, Brussels and Paris. London is served by a weekly flight from Gatwick which goes to Douala via Paris. Reconfirming flight tickets in Cameroon

for the return leg of your journey is absolutely essential – the flights are often overbooked.

Access to the Mountains

Mount Cameroon is extremely easy to get to from Douala, being about an hour's journey away by car. Buea is the town which serves as the base and there are plenty of hotels and guest houses there which cater for trekkers. Shared taxis run to Buea regularly from Douala, as do buses and minibuses.

The Mandara mountains are very remote, even by African standards. To get to them means either a long overland journey north from Douala or Yaounde, or hopping across the border from Nigeria or Chad if you happen to be in the region. Quite a few overland expeditions doing the London–Nairobi long-haul trips make a point of passing through the Mandara on the way south. Once in the area, it is relatively easy to get access to the Mandara. Using Maroua as the starting point, the mountains are within a day's travel using local trucks, shared taxis and whatever else turns up.

Language

In the south, around the Mount Cameroon area, quite a bit of English is spoken. Most of the guides on the mountain speak good English, French and German.

In the Mandara, French is widely spoken and some people also speak a few words of English.

Trekking Equipment

This is tropical Africa. Trekking gear should be lightweight and easy to dry in case of a sudden downpour. Humidity is likely to be a constant problem, and frequent changes of clothes are desirable when things get sweaty. Mount Cameroon can be extremely wet, so high-quality rain-gear is essential if the climb is made in the

A rare break in the cloud, Mount Cameroon.

rainy seasons. Waterproof trousers will help protect the legs from the soaked vegetation found
in the lower parts of the climb.

According to *The World Weather Guide* (*see*
Further Reading), the summit of Mount
Cameroon is one of three places in the world experiencing an average rainfall of more than
400in (10,000mm) per year. You have been
warned! Boots which offer some waterproofing
are an idea worth exploring.

Mount Cameroon is sufficiently high to get
fairly cold, and some thermal protection is a
good idea at this kind of altitude. The huts can
also be cold at night, so a reasonable sleeping
bag and karrimat are required.

The Mandara mountains lie in a far more arid
zone of West Africa. The climate varies from
hot and dry, to hot and wet! Apart from rain-
gear and good boots, lightweight shirts and
trousers will probably suffice.

Seasons

In the north, the year is split conveniently into
two roughly six-month seasons. The wet season
runs from April to September, whilst the dry
season occupies the rest of the year. Most people
avoid the wet season completely but walking in
the north is certainly possible all year round . . .
if you don't mind the discomfort of rain and
high humidity. The principal drawback of the
wet season is that roads and tracks may become
flooded and impassable, making travel slow and
difficult.

In the south, the possibility of heavy rain
exists nearly all year round but there are two

identifiable 'dry' seasons in the months of December and January, and in July and August. Humidity levels are as high as 97 per cent in the early morning, easing off as the day continues.

Guides

In both the walking areas described in this book, guides can easily be found. At Buea, the official government tourist office is on the left as you come into town. They will fix you up with guides and permits for the mountains. Dire consequences of prison and fines are threatened for those who are foolhardy enough to try the mountain on their own, or by an unauthorized route!

In the Mandara, the easiest place to find a guide is at the 'campement' at the village of Rhoumsiki.

Medical Advice

The possibility of illness deters many people from journeying to the tropics. Of all the dreaded lurgies, most of them can be found here in some shape or form. Yet, if you take sensible health precautions, there is no reason why you should get sick.

The key is to seek expert advice and take it seriously. Malaria is a good example. Far too many people take the tablets regularly at the start of the trip and then ignore the most important part of the course – taking them when they get home. Even if you don't see any mosquitoes, keep taking those malaria tablets. It only takes one infected mosquito to give you this very unpleasant disease.

Innoculations against other infectious diseases such as cholera, typhoid and yellow fever are amongst those that your doctor may recommend. I advise you to get all the injections on the prescribed list, which you can obtain from any medical centre. Note that entry to Cameroon is subject to a strict check of your international health certificate. You *must* have a valid stamp for yellow fever or they will try and inject you at the airport. This is *not* recommended for obvious reasons. The alternative may be that they will refuse you admission. Check with your nearest Cameroon embassy for details on up-to-date requirements for entry. On no account arrive at Douala airport without every piece of health documentation required.

The rest is really the sort of advice that holds true for travellers almost anywhere in the world. Eat only well-cooked food. Boil or purify all water. Where possible, cook your own food under conditions you know are hygenic.

Anti-fungal powders and mosquito repellent are useful additions to your kit, as is sun cream and lip protection.

Visas

Citizens of all countries require a visa for Cameroon. Check at your nearest embassy for details of requirements. A return air ticket, evidence of funds, health documents and letter of introduction are the minimum.

MALI

Getting There

Mali is a completely land-locked country bordered by Niger, Algeria, Mauritania, Senegal, Guinea, Ivory Coast and Burkina Faso. It is one of the principal countries on the main trans-Saharan routes to west Africa and many over-landers stop off at Timbuktu, Gao and Bandiagara on their way south. These are just some of the highlights of what must rate as one of the most interesting countries in Africa.

Bamako, the capital, is served by quite a few airlines. There are no direct flights from London but plenty of flights leave each week for Mali from Paris.

Market scene in Mali.

Access to the Bandiagara

The Bandiagara escarpment is situated not far from Mopti, one of Mali's main towns located on the banks of the river Niger. Getting to Mopti is a long and rough journey along mostly unpaved roads from Bamako or Gao if you are coming from the east. Bush taxis and commercial trucks regularly ply the route. There is an airport at Mopti which is served with internal flights from Bamako.

Language

A basic command of French is the best way to make yourself understood in Mali. English is not widely used here at all. If you have the time, a few words of local dialect will help for those times when you run out of people who speak any French.

Trekking Equipment

The extreme heat of summer in the Bandiagara dictates light and flexible clothing with plenty of layers to ward off the burning rays of the sun. Hat and sunglasses are, of course, essential. Water bottles should be carried at all times.

In winter months, when more visitors come, the days can be pleasantly warm, but the nights very chilly. Warm layers of jumper and anorak are advisable. Sleeping bags should be lightweight. A mosquito net might be a worthwhile investment.

Seasons

The northern parts of Mali stretch far into the Sahara desert and are virtually devoid of any rain. The south has infrequent rain from June through to about September. The annual inundation of the river Niger is the main source of water for cultivation. Winter months are cool right up to February but the spring months are extremely hot and dry. It is not advisable to plan summer expeditions to Mali unless you are experienced in these extreme conditions.

Guides

The Bandiagara has become increasingly popular for backpackers in the last few years and SMERT, the Mali tourist agency, have not been slow to capitalize on this. At Sangha, the main village for visiting the Dogon escarpment, the SMERT office will fix you up with guides and information but it is, for Mali, pretty expensive. Bandiagara village is the other logical place to pick up a guide.

Reports vary as to the powers of SMERT. Some people find they are virtually forced to pay government prices for their guide. Others hire an 'unofficial' guide much cheaper and report no problems with this. Seek advice from travellers in the area as to what the current situation is.

Medical

Your doctor will advise you on up-to-date requirements for innoculations. Check at the nearest Mali Embassy to you for their entry health regulations and make sure you have your International Vaccination certificate with you when arriving at the border.

Waterborne diseases and parasites are quite common in Mali and necessary precautions should be taken to ensure all food and water is uncontaminated. Malaria, dysentery, bilharzia

and hepatitis are all present in Mali and it is worth seeking specialist medical advice about how to avoid them.

Visas

Nationals of all countries except France need visas for Mali. There is no Mali Embassy in London. The Mali Embassy in Brussels is extremely friendly and efficient and issues visas to British passport holders normally within 48 hours. *See* Useful Addresses for their location.

MOROCCO

Getting There

The overland routes into Morocco mostly involve travelling down the length of Spain and then taking one of the many ferries that cross the Straits of Gibraltar to Tangiers or Ceuta. Ferries also operate from Marseilles in the south of France. Interail cards are valid for Morocco and this can be a cheap way to get there if you are young enough to qualify for the card.

There are plenty of cheap options by air if you look for charter deals from package operators. Agadir, Marrakesh and Tangiers are all served by these flights, particularly in the peak winter period. Some people just use the flight and ignore the accommodation but you could at least use the first and last nights of the stay if it is included in the price of the ticket. For the High Atlas mountains, the best option is to fly direct from London to Marrakesh. Royal Air Maroc offer this route at peak (winter) times of the year and their flights can be good value (*see* Useful Addresses at the end of the book for details).

The Anti Atlas, a good winter hiking area if you are reluctant to tackle possible deep snow and freezing conditions in the High Atlas, is very close to Agadir. A growing number of people are flying to Agadir on a cheap charter, staying on the beach for a week and then paying to extend their ticket so they can go walking in the Anti Atlas for the second week. Many people bring vehicles down into Morocco across Europe and this is another option if you have the time and money for a larger scale trip.

Access to the Mountains

Most of the suitable starting points for hikes in the High Atlas are easy to get to using local transport. Buses in Morocco are generally frequent and cheap. They are also painfully slow for the most part and often excruciatingly uncomfortable. The people you meet on board are almost always friendly and keen to chat. Be careful when you board the bus to make sure your rucksack is definitely on the roof-rack, and establish the going rate for luggage with a fellow passenger or you will be charged double or treble.

Where buses fear to tread you will find local trucks and 'bush taxis'. These are unpredictable in their movements and you may have to wait for a while. Market days are the best days for picking up lifts to obscure villages if you don't mind sharing a pick-up with a selection of nervous livestock. There are some regions of the High Atlas where you can wait for days for a vehicle but in general, if there is a road, you can get along it by some means, normally within a few hours.

Hitching lifts is sometimes possible but local trucks will always expect you to pay something. The only roads where there are sufficient tourist vehicles to give a good chance of hitchhiking are the road from Marrakesh across the Tizi 'n Tichka to Ouarzazate, and the route back again across the Tizi 'n Test.

Be warned that if you are planning a trek in the High Atlas in winter your plans may be altered radically by heavy snow. The main passes over the mountains are often closed at these times and you can find yourself unable to get near your proposed starting point with a vehicle. I have occasionally managed to get information on road closures by telephoning hotel managers in Marrakesh but this method is not always sure!

Language

You will find very little English is spoken in the mountains. It is advisable to speak enough basic French to get by with. Porters and guides invariably have their own local Berber dialects and mastering these is difficult. Learning a few words is enough to make friends with people.

Trekking Equipment

You must take all your gear out with you as virtually nothing is available for hire or purchase in the mountains. Imlil, being the main hiking centre for Toubkal, has a few shops which sell broken-down boots and the odd ice axe, but that's about it.

In summer, the ideal trekking equipment is lightweight and flexible. The days can be hot enough for shorts and T-shirt even above 10,000ft (3,000m). Down in the lower valleys it can get really hot. Be wary of wearing shorts (particularly women) in areas outside of the Toubkal region as these little-visited places are very conservative in their dress and you run the risk of offending people. Good strong boots capable of protecting your ankles against scree are essential. Take a minimum of 3.5pt (2 litres) of water whenever you set out as water supplies can be scarce. A thick jumper and lightweight rain jacket will protect you against cold nights and the risk of rain showers. A sunhat is useful.

In winter, do not underestimate the potential for really serious weather. Dress for the Alps and you can't go wrong. At the very least you need a good duvet jacket, wind- and waterproof layers on your head, hands and body, and thermal underwear which is useful at high altitudes.

Wear plenty of layers to adjust to changing conditions and have boots which can take crampons if you plan to walk on ice. Glacier goggles will protect the eyes from glare. A rope may be good if you are planning ambitious routes and an ice axe is essential for the bigger climbs.

Seasons

The most popular periods for walking in the High Atlas are in the spring and autumn. This is the time when the rivers are generally running well and the air temperature is moderate and fresh. In April and May, the lower slopes are covered with wonderful flowers and plants and the air is alive with butterflies and exotic insects like the curious hummingbird hawkmoth. In the height of summer, the heat can make walking very unpleasant until fairly high up in the mountains. The Anti Atlas is most frequently visited in winter, but hiking there is also possible throughout spring and autumn. Summer in the Anti Atlas is as hot as one would expect for a range of mountains which borders the Sahara Desert.

Guides, Porters and Mules

The tracks in the High Atlas are normally well defined and many backpackers strike out with just a map. If you do want a guide, you will not find it difficult to find one, wherever you are in the High Atlas. The villages are packed with prospective guides who will go with you, often at a moment's notice, for a reasonable fee. They are usually excellent people, as tough as old boots, and know the mountains intimately. The real advantage is that when you arrive at a village your guide will know someone you can stay with and arrange a personal introduction. This is always better than turning up and hoping that someone will take you in for the night.

Porters are also easy to find, and are useful if you are in a big group which is planning a long hike where supplies will be difficult to purchase on the way. Again, these Berbers are incredibly strong, cheerful and honest. In all my wanderings in the mountains of Morocco I have never witnessed any act that changed my high opinion of the Berbers. I have known people to leave cameras on rocks after a drink-stop, to then find them returned by Berbers who have hurried after them on a mule.

Mules are good pack-animals and can take two rucksacks with ease. They can tackle the highest passes and cost little to hire. Hiring one or two can make a hike much more pleasant. They come with a muleteer and a price should be negotiated in advance.

Staying in Villages

The most interesting hikes to be done in Morocco are the ones that link together remote villages. There is normally someone in any village who will be willing to give some floor space to incoming walkers. You have to be way off the beaten track to find a village where this practice is not recognized . . . but you also must not take it for granted.

The Berbers are by nature incredibly hospitable, but hikers should always bear in mind that when they eat with their host they are diminishing the precious resources of the village. Many times I have seen a chicken killed and cooked for a meal to celebrate the arrival of a stranger. It all seems so easy until you look around and realize that the two or three chickens the family has left are the end of their meat supply. As a result, no matter how strongly the host may protest, a small gift of money is an excellent idea. At least then you have replaced the resource you have used. I have found that a good way of achieving the sometimes impossible task of giving a small amount of money to a host is to carry some envelopes. Put the money in an envelope and tell your host not to open it until you have gone!

Kasbah in the southern High Atlas mountains of Morocco.

The second option on food is to take all of your own and cook it yourself. This is far more preferable from the point of view of time and medical concerns but if you really want to get to know the Berbers, you have to eat with them.

Permits and Huts

The High Atlas and Anti Atlas have no official bodies controlling them or who require a permit for hiking. The mountain huts of the Club Alpin Français (CAF) are to be found in the Toubkal area and provide excellent bases to attempt some of the higher peaks. The rates per night are cheaper if you are a member of the club, but non-members are welcome to stay at a slightly higher nightly rate. These huts can be very crowded (particularly the Neltner hut for

the Toubkal ascent) at peak times of the year like April and May.

Medical Advice

By far the biggest problems suffered in the mountains of Morocco are gastro-intestinal upsets. The risk of these increases if you eat in the villages, where hygiene is often a totally unknown concept. Often, your village host will proudly display the washing-up bowl to show you that the plates are clean. Well they are, but he then dries them on a rag which harbours several million types of germ and has not been washed for ages. It really is hard to know what to do in these circumstances. My technique was to look at the family and see how healthy they looked. If they glowed with health I would eat

123

the lot! If they looked like death I would make my excuses. Needless to say, this is a ridiculous system and I often got sick, but never so that it interfered with the trekking or my enjoyment of it. If you take the time to acclimatize, you will probably be able to eat as the locals do.

There are some nasty infections to watch out for. Hepatitis is quite common in some areas and an injection of gamma-globulin might give you some protection against this. If you see someone who is very obviously carrying the disease (often they are yellow-skinned) be careful not to eat food they might prepare. Don't even think about eating uncooked food unless it really is prepared by someone you know is taking some hygenic measures to stop the risk of infections.

Stream water is safe to drink where it is obviously straight from the source, but do not drink water from a stream which has a village further upstream unless you boil it or purify it first. Even if there is no village further up, take care. The water may have gone through a whole variety of terraced fields which might be fertilized with the most unsavoury types of dung!

A good medical kit is indispensable. Bandages, sun cream and lip moisturizer will be in frequent demand. A supply of aspirins is useful. Villagers will 'raid' your medical supplies for basics, so take plenty. If you are not medically trained, do not offer medical treatment to people with a problem unless you really know what you are doing.

Above 10,000ft (3,000m) the risk of altitude sickness is always present. If you take the time to acclimatize, this should present no problem but if you do feel the effects of high altitude, the best cure is to descend rapidly and recover at lower levels.

Visas

British citizens do not at present require visas to enter Morocco but it is worth checking with your nearest embassy before you go as to the current requirements.

Maps

Stanford's map shop in London is the best source of maps for the High Atlas and many other regions of Morocco, although their supply can be variable depending on demand. There are good 1:100,000 maps produced in Rabat which are ideal for hiking purposes and cover most of the popular areas. In Paris, at the IGN, a more comprehensive collection can be found. Be aware that some of the 1:100,000 maps of the High Atlas have major discrepancies lurking within them. Non-existent villages and invisible tracks are amongst the horrors!

Organized Tours

There are several companies who offer organized hiking tours of the High Atlas and Anti Atlas. One good way of finding them is to look in the small ads pages of the *Sunday Times* travel section, or in publications like *Time Out* or *Private Eye*. Explore Worldwide and Exodus both have established programmes with inclusive packages from the UK or 'local' packages if you want to get there under your own steam and then join the group for the hike.

Further Reading

GENERAL INFORMATION AND GUIDE-BOOKS

Crowther, G., *Africa on a Shoestring*, (Lonely Planet, 1988).

Else, D., *Backpacker's Africa*, (Bradt Publications, 1988).

Oliver, R. and Atmore, A., *Africa since 1800*, (Cambridge University Press, 1981).

Pearce, E.A. and Smith, C.G., *The World Weather Guide*, (Hutchinson, 1990).

Wexas, *The Traveller's Handbook*, (Futura, 1988).

MOROCCO

Chatinières, P., *Dans les Grands Atlas Marocains*, (PLON, 1919).

Clarke, B., *Berber Village*, (Longman, 1959).

Collomb, R., *Atlas Mountains*, (West Col Productions, 1980).

Crane, N., *Atlas Biker*, (Oxford Illustrated Press, 1990).

Fougerolles, A., *Le Haut Atlas Central*, (IDEALE, 1982).

Harris, W. B., *Tafilet*, (William Blackwood and Sons, 1895).

Harris, W.B., *Morocco That Was*, (William Blackwood and Sons, 1921).

Maxwell, G., *Lords of the Atlas*, (Arrow, 1991).

Smith, K., *The Atlas Mountains — A Walker's Guide*, (Cicerone Press, 1989).

ALGERIA

Durou, J. – M., *Sahara — Magic Desert*, (Arpel Graphics, 1986).

Foucauld, Père C. de, *Dictionnaire Touareg–Francais (4 volumes)*, (Imprimerie Nationale de France, 1951).

Fremantle, A., *Desert Calling — The Life of Charles de Foucauld*, (Hollis and Carter, 1950).

Glen, S. and J., *Sahara Handbook*, (Roger Lascelles, 1980).

Lhote, H., *The Search for the Tassili Frescoes*, (J. Susse, 13 Rue de Grenelle, Paris 7^e, 1958).

Sheppard, T., *Desert Expeditions*, (Expedition Advisory Centre, 1988).

Stevens, V. and J., *Algeria and the Sahara — A Handbook for Travellers*, (Constable, 1977).

CAMEROON

Barley, N., *A Plague of Caterpillars*, (Penguin, 1986).

Barley, N., *The Innocent Anthropologist*, (Penguin, 1986).

Daniels, A., *Zanzibar to Timbuktu*, (Century Hutchinson, 1989).

Deane, S., *Talking Drums — From a Village in Cameroon*. (John Murray, 1985).

Kingsley, M., *Travels in West Africa*, (Virago, 1982).

Murphy, D., *Cameroon with Egbert*, (Longmans, 1988).

Serle, W., Morel, G. J., Hartwig, W., *A Field Guide to the Birds of West Africa*, (Collins, 1988).

MALI

Africanus, L., *History and Description of Africa*, (Hakluyt Society, 1896).

Alexander, J., *Whom the Gods Love — Boyd Alexander's Expedition from the Niger to the Nile*, (William Heinemann Ltd., 1977).

Asher, M., *Impossible Journey*, (Viking, 1988).

Lee, Reverend S. (Translator), *The Travels of Ibn Batuta*, (Burt Franklin, 1971).

Moorhouse, G., *The Fearful Void*, (Penguin, 1986).

Norris, H.T., *The Touaregs — Their Islamic Legacy and its Diffusion in the Sahel*, (Aris and Phillips Ltd., 1975).

Park, M., *Travels into the Interior of Africa*, (Eland Books, 1983).

Tench, R., *Forbidden Sands*, (John Murray, 1978).

Useful Addresses

Embassy of the Republic of Mali,
487 Avenue Molière
1060 Bruxelles,
Belgium

Algerian Embassy,
54 Holland Park
London W11

6 Hyde Park Gate,
London SW7

(Tel: 071 228 7800)

(Tel: 071 581 4260)

Air Algérie,
10 Baker Street,
London W1

(Tel: 071 487 5903)

Cameroon Embassy,
84 Holland Park,
London W11

(Tel: 071 727 0771)

Cameroon Airlines,
44 Conduit Street,
London W1

(Tel: 071 734 7676)

Moroccan Embassy,
49 Queens Gate Gardens,
London SW7

(Tel: 071 581 5001)

Royal Air Maroc,
174 Regent Street,
London W1

(Tel: 071 439 4361)

Index